My Walk Past Hell

By Dr. Yolanda Jerry

Published By: Tamika INK

Library of Congress Cataloging – in- Publication Data has been applied for.

ISBN: 9798502607827

PRINTED IN THE UNITED STATES OF AMERICA.

Dedication

This book is dedicated to my late father,
Willie James Jones (1950-2017).

I know you are in heaven and are so proud of me. I want to thank
you for all the teachings and wisdom you poured into. Showing me
right from wrong and most of all encouraging me in my faith walk.
Everything I do now is because of the positive influence you have
had on my life. The family and the lives you have touched miss you
so much, but I know you are at peace and no longer suffering.
You said to me in your last days, "Yolanda don't stop what you have
a passion for, I'll always be here." I find these words to be true.
I will continue to carry you in my heart and make you proud.
I love you and miss you!

Love,
Your oldest daughter,
Dr. Yolanda Jerry

Acknowledgements

I thank God for giving me the vision and courage to step out on faith to bring this anthology to life. You have been my source of strength my entire life and I am grateful. May you get all the glory because without you, there would be no me!

To my mother, Rumualda C. Jones, I thank you for always supporting me and shown me what strength looks like. Besides dad, you have been my biggest supporter, nurturer and I am blessed to be your daughter. I love you!

To my daughter, Imari Smith, you are God's gift to me. You are the reason why I continue to live and work hard each day. Thank you for your unconditional love and believing me always. I love you!

To the MY WALK PAST HELL contributing authors, the editor, the book cover design artist, family and friends who played a role in this anthology journey. I thank you for the love, support, trust, integrity and transparency along the way. May God bless each one of you!

Table of Contents

A Message from The Visionary Author

When you think of the title *MY WALK PAST HELL*, what do you think about? Let us look at the word *HELL* itself. In religion, *HELL* is an afterlife location where evil souls are subjected to punitive suffering, often torture, as eternal punishment after death. Well, truth be told, many people experience hell on earth. As a survivor of domestic violence and sexual assault, I have had to walk past hell a couple of times.

If 2020 has taught us anything, it was that you can be either in the midst of or walking right past hell at any given moment. People had obstacles, hardships, pains, traumas, or sufferings but still had to push through. My new anthology will help bring attention to women who have endured it all and are now walking in their purpose. As a servant leader, I wanted to create a platform to allow individuals to share their very personal hell story and show how, by God's grace, they are still here to share it with the world unapologetically.

I have served alongside some of these women, mentored a few, and even met some for the first time because of this project... these phenomenal women are RESILIENT and UNSINKABLE. All their stories will definitely be LIFE-CHANGING for those individuals who read them. Listen…*MY WALK PAST HELL ANTHOLOGY* is bringing a whole new TRANSFORMATIONAL energy in 2021 and beyond.

As a woman who advocates for men and women who suffer in silence, I encourage you to decide you will no longer be held in bondage. Now is your time to walk past hell. Begin your healing journey today. Seek God in prayer and reach out to others to help you along the way. NO MORE SUFFERING IN SILENCE. Your MY WALK PAST HELL journey with us begins now. I hope you enjoy reading the stories in this book. Many of them are sharing their stories for the first time. Thank you for joining us on this journey. Love and blessings to you!!!

Your Visionary Author,

Dr. Yolanda Jerry

www.iamyolandajerry.com

Foreword

by Dr. Marsie Ross

Dr. Yolanda Jerry carries with her the type of strength you instinctively know comes from surviving something that would put most people on a downward spiral. She never has to tell you the hell she went through for you to know she's a survivor. When I first met Dr. Jerry, her quiet presence and inner peace drew me like a magnet. I remember like it was yesterday. As a woman with my own story of being lost and found, we were sharing our life's journey during the same international women's conference in London. I remember feeling awestruck as she openly shared how she lived through the hell of domestic violence. But more than her story, it was her willingness to offer herself as a source of inspiration for anyone finding themselves in a similar circumstance. I remember her saying, "If I can find my way out on the other side, so can you." The authenticity oozed out of her! This is the woman leading this masterpiece you are about to receive. On the surface, each chapter may feel like a tragic story, but these women are far from victims of their experiences. They are here to bear witness, so you can absolutely know there's a way for you too. So read their story and feel their pain but make sure that you feel their triumph.

I've been a healthcare professional for more than 30 years, and as a clinician and integrative nutrition health coach, I often meet women at a place in their lives that they'd rather not be. More often than not, they've lost sight of their confidence and of the woman they feel proud to be. It's because of my own lived experiences and past struggles with self-care, self-sabotage, and a self-limited mindset regarding my wellness that I allow myself to be the best fit to guide them and to see them fully. And it's this same guiding principle that allows these women before to share so openly with you. Life comes with many peaks and valleys. And these rolling hills can seem to come from nowhere. It's human to want to push down the memories of when we were abused emotionally, mentally, or physically. The memories when we were not in control of what was done to us. When others did not protect us, and if you have walked this path, this is exactly why you must press on and read this powerful book. The lived experience of so many women in one book will serve as a powerful reminder of your own inner strength. You are a victor! You are not alone! Your pain is only part of your story.

About Dr. Marsie Ross

Dr. Marsie Ross "The Women's Health Hero" is a Women's Health Expert, Award-Winning Clinical Pharmacist, Certified Integrative Nutrition Health Coach, international author, speaker and has been featured on multiple national platforms, including NBC, ABC and The Huffington Post. Dr. Marsie is the founder of Healthy and Happy Coaching, an elite firm dedicated to the health advancement of women. After several years of private health coaching, Dr. Marsie answered the call to use her superpowers to cultivate a community where women over 40 could thrive. The Wellness Academy for Women is designed to be just that! The core pillars of the academy are to educate, empower and energize for maximum and lasting health benefits. Dr. Marsie uses her signature E3 Method to help community members learn how to infuse healthy habits into their everyday busy lives so they can be consistent and intentional. As a wife, mother of 3, and CEO, Dr. Marsie understands how important both encouragement and accountability are for women who are on a path to creating a lifelong relationship with nutrition and exercise. Dr. Marsie is unapologetically living to help women, just like you, be the hero of their own story!

Follow Dr. Marsie on Clubhouse, FaceBook and Instagram
@DrMarsie

My Innocence Was Taken Away From Me

by Dr. Yolanda Jerry

*I*f you have followed the "MeToo" Movement, you'll know this movement has had a lot of attention. More women are coming forward now about their experiences. This movement was originally started in 2007 by a woman named Tarana Burke to let women of color, who survived sexual assault, know they were not alone. Actress Alyssa Milano started using the hashtag #MeToo, and since then, it has gone viral and is now a movement. The actress also credited Ms. Burke as the creator and called the story "heartbreaking" and "inspiring."

Nationally April is Sexual Assault Awareness Month. At the young age of 13 years old, I was molested by a man who was considered a family friend. This man was my dad's best friend, and he touched me in places a man should never touch a child. He did things and engaged me sexually in ways that adults engage with other adults. What this man did to me did not feel good at all. He fondled my little breasts, kissed me all over my body, stuck his fingers and penis in my vagina. It was very painful. All I could do was lay there in silence and cry. What he did to me made me feel dirty, used, and lost. Most of all, I lost virginity to a man I looked up to as an uncle.

So just imagine the thoughts in my head at this age. I was afraid to say anything to anyone. My molester told me that he would kill me and my family members if I ever spoke of what he did to me. Of course, I was terrified, so I kept quiet and kept this secret to myself. My innocence was taken away from me! Although it was only a one-time incident, it was an extremely traumatic experience for me as a teenager. Five years later, when I turned 18 years old, I left for Air Force Basic Training. I knew by leaving; I would rarely ever have to see this man again. At least that was my hope. Even after I had left, I still never said anything to my dad. Why? Because my dad was a police officer. I knew for a fact my dad would have killed that man.

A few years went by, and at 22 years old, I learned that my molester had passed away. In that moment, I felt relieved, but it still did not take away the fact that I was a victim of sexual assault who was molested as a child. This was something I would always remember and must live with for the rest of my life. This experience has affected my life in a way where I was and still am very over-protective of my daughter and who I let around her. But as she grew up through her years, I did my best to keep an open, communicative relationship with my daughter and teach her to be aware of molesters, pedophiles, and other things about life she should be aware of. Today, my daughter is 21 years old, and I thank God she has not experienced what I had been through.

Having served an additional duty as a Sexual Assault Victim Advocate for 12 years until I retired, I felt it was my duty to help victims and let them know they were not alone. Now, after retirement, I still choose to be an advocate for others. I am all too familiar with the devastating impacts of sexual assault and the stigma that some survivors experience. If you are a survivor of sexual assault, here are three things that I want you to know according to what I've read, and I also know from experience.

1. **What happened to you was not your fault.**

    I know you may have heard this before, but that it might be difficult for you to believe. You may think to yourself, "If only I hadn't gone to that party, this wouldn't have happened," or "I chose to go back to his room, so it was my fault for sending him mixed signals."

    First off, I want you to know that this is a common reaction to sexual trauma. Your mind wants to make sense of a situation that ultimately was out of your control. Therefore, many people wrongly believe that they must have been responsible for what happened to them.

The reality is that when someone is sexually assaulted, the only person who is to blame is the perpetrator. No matter what party you went to if you had a drink, if you didn't fight the person off, if you were dating the person, if you were aroused, and regardless of any other circumstance, it was not your fault. You were not responsible for this, and you certainly did not deserve it.

If you are struggling with feelings of GUILT and SHAME following sexual trauma, it can be incredibly helpful to reach out to a psychotherapist (preferably one who specializes in trauma).

2. **Healing takes time, but it is absolutely possible.**

There are many stages of healing following trauma, and everyone copes with this process differently. It's important to note, healing and coping with the impact of a traumatic experience can take time, but it is completely possible to get to a place where you are able to have healthy relationships, rebuild a sense of trust and security, and find meaning and purpose in your life.

It's important to be compassionate with yourself for whatever emotions you are experiencing. Beating yourself up for feeling the way that you do will likely only cause you to feel worse. You went through something that no one should have to endure, and you are certainly not alone in struggling with the aftermath of trauma. Ultimately, you deserve to treat yourself with the same kindness that you would give to a loved one who had experienced trauma.

No one should have to struggle with this alone. Reaching out for support from professionals, as well as friends and loved ones, can be incredibly helpful for survivors. Even if they can't completely understand how you are feeling. They can provide you with love and support when you are struggling.

3. **It's healthy and "ok" to feel the feelings you have.**

After trauma, there is often a sense of wanting to be "numb." Survivors might turn to negative coping mechanisms, such as drinking, using drugs, not eating, or self-inflicting wounds, to try to escape their intense emotions. Know that these coping mechanisms are coming from a good place, as you are using them in an attempt to feel better. But keep in mind that these strategies only provide temporary relief and often lead to greater emotional pain in the long term.

Engaging in these behaviors can cause you to become dependent on them. In addition, as human beings, we are unable to selectively numb emotions. When we numb ourselves from feeling anxious and depressed, we also block ourselves from feeling LOVE, PEACE, AND JOY.

It is ok and healthy to allow yourself to feel your feelings. Emotions are like waves in the ocean. They rise and peak, but ultimately if you allow yourself to sit with them, they will decrease in intensity. Talking to a therapist, counselor, and/or life coach when you feel emotionally overwhelmed is one healthy way to process your feelings. Other ways might include talking to loved ones, journaling, drawing, going to a support group, or reaching out to a helpline.

Final Thoughts

Yes, my innocence was taken away from me, but it pushed me into my purpose. No matter the words that are playing around in your mind, understand, YOU DID NOTHING WRONG. No one deserves to be molested and/or sexually assaulted. In no way was it your fault. You have had a traumatic experience in life, but you are in control of your healing journey right now. Love yourself enough to turn your trauma into your TRIUMPH. Seek God in prayer daily and surround yourself with people who will love you despite your past. And lastly, ensure you educate and bring awareness to the community and those around you. Remember, SEXUAL ASSAULT IS NOT OKAY! God bless you!

About Dr. Yolanda Jerry

Advocacy is centered at the heart of every Philanthropist. Echoing that notion at its finest is the diversified professional, Dr. Yolanda Jerry.

Dr. Yolanda Jerry is a Best-Selling Author, speaker, business guru, and CEO and Founder of YJ Empowerment Solutions LLC and YJ Inspires, a multidisciplinary advocacy program, invented to help clients push beyond their past traumas, and elevate to the next level, both personally and professionally. Affectionately known as the "Empowerment Advocate", Dr. Jerry is reputed for her innate ability to exhort multigenerational audiences through her powerful and relatable messages; as she passionately advocates for truth, healing, resiliency, and personal growth. Yolanda delivers an awe-inspiring proponent perspective against domestic violence, youth bullying, and sexual assault. Through the vernacular of a survivor, she impacts many; inspiring them to create the best version of themselves; despite tragedy, and to become intentional, in the pursuit of their life's purpose and goals.

Yolanda's mantra is simple: Accept the past. Focus on the now. Impact the future.

Adding to her philanthropic capacity, Dr. Yolanda Jerry is also a retired Air Force veteran and Co-Founder of **Bridging The Gap Transitional Age Youth Program**. As a highly respected member of both local and national community, Yolanda has been featured and headlined in well-respected publications, such as: the **Huffington Post, Sheen Magazine, Glambitious Magazine, Courageous Woman Magazine, MizCEO Entrepreneurial Magazine, Gulf Coast Woman Magazine, Success Women's Magazine** and many more; all highlighting the remarkable impression Yolanda has left on an ever changing world. One of Yolanda's most celebrated features was an article she wrote called "The Day I Decided to Leave". A compelling survivor's testament so impressive, it was chosen by highly respected serial producer and screenwriter, Shonda Rhimes, to be displayed in her online storytelling periodical column, "Shondaland" in 2020.

Dr. Jerry is also recognized as both a highly decorated professional and nonprofit organizer, receiving numerous awards and recognition, for her contributions to charity, business, military service, and community. She is the proud recipient of the **Humanitarian Service Award: Trinity International University of Ambassadors** (June 2018), the **Rising Star Award: Mississippi Gulf Coast Black Owned Businesses** (Feb 2019), **"You Are Beautiful" Survivor Award & State of Connecticut Official Citation** (sep2019), **One Coast Community Leader Award Finalist: Mississippi Gulf Coast Chamber of Commerce** (Jan2020), **Top 50 Black Women in Business in Mississippi: Black Women's Business Expo** (Jan2020), **Volunteer of the Year and Top Influencer Award: Success Women's Conference** (Oct2020), and many more. Yolanda currently holds chair on over 14 well respected community organizations, attesting candidly, to the force she is in the arenas of business and servant leadership.

When Dr. Yolanda Jerry is not out advocating for those in need. She is a loving partner, mother, and friend.

Dr. Yolanda Jerry. | Leader. | Energizer. | Advocate.
Website: http://www.iamyolandajerry.com
Business email: yolanda@yjempowers.com

Death Couldn't Have Me

by Kearn Cherry

The day started with just another nosebleed that would eventually last all day and night. Nosebleeds have been a part of my life since I was a little girl. When I started having nosebleeds because of my medication, coumadin, it was just another life adjustment. I had been taking coumadin for almost 10 years because my body was producing blood clots. You see, I had been living with pulmonary hypertension for years at this point. Though the disease seems like a death sentence, I was not going to let it slow me down. So, I continued with my busy pace of running several businesses, volunteering, and running events just to name a few things. This nosebleed was just another roadblock that I was going to conquer.

I decided that day, I wasn't going to even miss church. My daughter was visiting, and it was a good day to go. As night fell, I was still bleeding. My husband decided to check on me. As I got up, I slowly passed out. Seeming unresponsive, my daughter who was a medical student, called for help and my husband prayed. My husband thought I was gone but he wasn't willing to give up. I truly believe his prayers brought me back. As my husband explained to the medics that this was all caused by nosebleeds, my body released a liter and half of blood again. I was going fast. It all became a blur as the hospital tried to pump me full of blood and send me to another hospital. Death could not have me yet, but it wasn't finished trying.

I would return to the hospital exactly a week later because death was trying to take me again. I had lost another liter and half of blood and this time they could not find my blood type. As I sat in the hospital waiting, death was always near. I knew it because I was not bouncing back. You see, my blood pressure was slowly dropping, and the hospital had to admit they could not find my blood type. Every day a doctor would try to figure out why I was still losing blood. My husband was becoming more concerned that they did not have any solutions. He even suggested transferring me to UAB Hospital. But GOD! I felt that death was circling me. The trip would be too long, so I decided to stay put. Then God sent me a message through yet another doctor. A familiar face that I wasn't expecting. He sent a doctor who had been trained at UAB. That was my sign to know that He was there, and He still had a purpose for me. Though I continued to lose blood, I knew that today's death was not going to win. The sign had been sent and a message was received.

As I continued on the journey, death still never gave up. My blood pressure decided to drop extremely low one more time, but God showed me that corporate prayer is effective. My husband called on the church to pray and I called on all of my women of faith within an hour and death was blocked once again. It was as if I had never lost a drop of blood. I felt GREAT! I could get up and dance, but as you probably guess, death wasn't done. I have pulmonary hypertension. Anything that challenges my oxygen level can put me to sleep forever. I had one more hurdle to overcome, a procedure that required me to be put in a light sleep. Any type of anesthesia can be life-threatening for a person with pulmonary hypertension. After the procedure, death tried one more time as my oxygen took a deep dive in the 70s.

As I walked through that journey and looked back, I know that God was there the whole time. You see, death has tried to take me a few times, but as a servant of the Lord, Jehovah, He has kept me. I could have given up on many occasions, but I know that I serve a purpose. Death can't have me, and it certainly can't hold me from my God-given purpose.

If you are on the brink of death, prayers can help you walk right by. Don't be afraid to call on others to help you through. You see, where two or three come together in prayer, God is always there. Never let death win. If you find yourself in the grips of death, call on Jesus. He will pull you through. I am a living testimony that death can't keep you!

About Kearn Cherry

Speaker, best-selling author, and award-winning businesswoman, Kearn Crockett Cherry, is a female tycoon with a "leg-up" in successful entrepreneurship. Laying to rest any stigma surrounding the stagnancy of female leadership in the Deep South, Kearn has enjoyed more than two decades of excellence, as the CEO of a thriving health care business on the Gulf Coast of Mississippi.

Kearn hosts a portfolio holding countless awards, acknowledging her abilities; locally, nationally, and internationally. She is a recognized figure in both business and communal leadership, holding membership and chair positions on diverse councils and local organizations.

While cherishing a well-earned reputation in business, it has been her ability to gather the masses that classifies Kearn Cherry, as a household name.

The Success Women's Conference is an award winning- business leadership conference attracting an annual audience of over 17,000 attendees worldwide. Les Brown, Dr. Iyanla Vanzant, Lisa Nichols, and Robin Roberts are some of the few "powerhouses" to take center stage; leaving Kearn Cherry and her contributing partners with a reputation for revolutionizing the way women interpret both public speaking and business, on a global scale.

In 2001, Kearn Cherry effortlessly graced the pages of one of the most popular publications in the world, **Essence Magazine**. Featured in both their local, and international publications; Kearn was recognized as the "**Comeback Queen**", confirming her commitment to exemplify dynamic business agility. Today, Kearn is a familiar face on several Magazine covers, all testifying to the *entrepreneurial giant,* she truly is. Out of many publications highlighting her expertise; **Speakers Magazine, Sheen Magazine**, and her very own, **Power-Up Speakers Edition Magazine**; are amongst her favorites.

Proving to be an unshakable force for over 25 years, Kearn Cherry has been blessed with an ability to integrate the outstanding professional ethics she acquired throughout her generation, and seamlessly translate its importance, to *rising* millennial audiences.

In 2020, Kearn facilitated her very own business-networking platform.

Giving birth to Amazon best-selling book; **<u>Trailblazers Who Lead: Unsung Heroes</u>**, a manuscript comprising 29 stories featuring several well-respected female entrepreneurs, moguls, and business professionals. In the midst of its release, Kearn also facilitated two innovative web-conferences: the "**Level-Up Your Visibility Virtual Summit**" and the "**Power up Summit**". Both by which, featured the best of multi-generational entrepreneurs, influencers, authors, and business professionals; all offering top-tier advice, recommendations, and business exhortation to professionals, entrepreneurial hopefuls, and those facing the unforeseen challenge in maintaining a successful business during a global crisis.

Enthusiastic about the future, Kearn remains diligent in helping entrepreneurs reach their destined potential. She is currently creating a book anthropology titled; "Make It Happen", a manuscript dedicated to those with an unyielding resilience to succeed; *a quality Kearn Cherry embodies all too well.* She will follow up with "Trailblazers Who Lead II".

kearn@prnhomecareservices.com www.kearncherry.com

Hail RaiZer: Pain to Praise

by Mavis A. Creagh

What does it look like to bottle up Satan in a glass and have it engulfed with flames from hell bursting into 1,000 pieces? Do you choke on the smoke or crawl through the fire?

The analogy for my life…my journey. Many times, I have been in cycles of hurt, harm, and danger; like a combustible gas trapped in an unstable containment unit. On top of this, an issue enters the environment and acts as a spark. The situation that was barely being handled now covers me in a spontaneous eruption. My heart was consumed with anguish and my soul was overtaken by a volatile explosion that was sent to delete my purpose, promise, and future.

I have had to endure terrible things throughout my life. There were times when I genuinely believed the enemy was aiming to fully destroy me. Living as a walking zombie with deadened emotion in order not to be devoured by the inferno. Wondering aimlessly through heavy smog in a smoldering deathtrap as my mind became weaker. My throat being preverbally choked as the enemy trampled on my voice.

Sitting catatonic in my spirit. **Screaming** internally with no sound. **Soul** bleeding from the inside out.

My experience involves neglect, torture, and degrading treatment. For almost 10 years, I was involved with someone whom I felt would be my lifelong mate. I believed that things would work out and that I could prove my worth in exchange for love. I am a survivor of multiple forms of abuse, self-hatred, low self-esteem, and poor life choices.

I have shared some of my life story before, but never in detail and with the emotion and effects on me as a person. Abuse can kill the spirit, mind, heart, and soul! Every day I am thankful for my life and sanity. Things could have truly gone another way and I am reminded why it is important to be transparent because it may save someone's life!

My goal in sharing my testimony is not to humiliate but to encourage anyone that is going through abuse or who has been removed from the abusive situation to walk boldly to their "Next." The title, "Walk Past Hell" resonated with me because I have seen Satan and stared death in the face.

Many times, abusers will dangle promises, more love, or consistency when in actuality they are being led by Satan. He has no respect for your future, family, or faith. His goal is to strip you down to nothing and hold you, hostage, in a burning inferno if you allow him.

The promise that I know is, that even in hell, there is hope! Even through the fire, there is life and means of escape. No matter how low you may have been or how long you have been held down, remind yourself that you are loved and that you matter to the Creator.

My situation did not start with slaps, threats, or shame. However, it did start without clear intentions or wholeness. Truly, how a relationship starts is a strong indicator of how it will develop. Often there are warning signs that could save years of soul-crushing trauma. One of my most vivid memories was yelling out crying and telling my abuser that, "I didn't deserve this" as I was being struck repeatedly for trying to speak up for myself. To beg someone continuously, and still not have a voice, is one of the worst feelings in the world. Now, I try to give a voice to survivors and people who are suffering from abuse.

My voice now is a quiet storm! Every time I speak, I envision myself like the character "Storm" on the X-Men…creating Hail in a good way after going through Hell. Every time I open my mouth and speak to audiences, share my story, write, create plays, manifest strategic plans, produce my show, give another woman hope… I am the quiet storm that Satan tried to kill.

I know my abuser did not expect me to stay the course. I have been no contact for over 2 years after a 10-year relationship. We were not legally married, but the goal was to be together and married as best friends. I remember having a discussion with him before being forced to leave the house. I stated he was my best friend and asked myself what was I going to do? He stated I was never his and this hurt at the time more than the abuse. However, I now know this was true because you do not purposely tear people down that you love. That is not the design of the Most High. I know some people say everyone is different, but different does not equal mistreatment.

If anyone is experiencing any form of abuse, there is help and you can survive on your own. The Father does not want his children to suffer day in and day out for the sake of false gods or corrupted love. The enemy is cunning and will use people, places, and materialistic standards to entrap you in a situation (relationship, friendship, work environment) that will kill you from the inside out. I remember a time when I was told something that made me feel ugly, unwanted, and unworthy. As I was crying and looking into the mirror, I hollered out in anguish and began to pull at my own hair. Because he had made me feel worthless, I in turn was reacting as the ignited flame in an already toxic situation. Now that I think about the jarring memory, I laugh at myself because I did not even have enough hair to pull. (I always try to use humor to lighten up my situations). I think this was around the time I became fixated on death, severely depressed, and suicidal. I was close to having a mental breakdown and even prayed once as a bargaining chip to God to take my mind since He would not allow me to kill myself. What must have been the depths of my anguish to try and use my mind as a bargaining tool? I have been asked before what it was like to live through my previous situation and the answer simply **"Hell"**!

Whatever Hell you endured, remember, you made it out when a lot of other people did not. This is what I remind myself on days that I have flashbacks and emotions that try and take over my mind. I am grateful for those who support me and do not judge. I believe in therapy, counseling, and understand healing is a process. I am truly thankful because I could have been on the news and my son could have been without a mother. I could have lost my mind in the midst of my pain. I could have returned to alcoholism to cope or I could have snapped and turned to violence while doing something that I would have regretted for the rest of my life. But God…He kept me and is restoring me even more. Daily, I pray for healing and restoration from the internal scars of the fire. I pray for anyone who has gone through abuse in any form and those who are currently living in Hell.

May **Peace**, **Protection**, and **Provision** be your **Portion**.

Even when your soul cries from memories of despair and anguish, remember **who** and **whose** you are.

Not **Trash** but a **Treasure** worth more than rubies and diamonds. **Sons** and *Daughters* of the **Most High**!

From my experiences, I have seen the best and worst of people and myself. I remain hopeful even after attacks on my mind, body, and spirit. The Creator is ever-present and wants nothing but the best for me and His children. Even when being attacked, stripped of spirit, and degraded, I believe in **restoration!** I know without question that there is nothing too hard for our divine Creator. I was broken to my core and felt exposed by the attacks. However, I remain resolute in my faith and have unwavering assurance in the Most High.

> *For I am convinced that neither death nor life, neither angels nor demons, neither the present nor the future, nor any powers, neither height nor depth, nor anything else in all creation, will be able to separate us from the love of God that is in Christ Jesus our Lord. Romans 8:38-39 (NIV)*

*With all the **Journeys** through **Storms** that were meant to break me.*
*The Fires of Hell (**Spontaneous Combustion**) still did not consume ME!!!*
Flying High Creating My Own Storm
*A True "**Hail RaiZer**"!*

> *"For I know the plans I have for you," says the Lord. "They are plans for good and not for disaster, to give you a future and a hope. Jeremiah 29:11 (NLT)*

About Mavis A. Creagh

Mavis A. Creagh is a best-selling author, speaker, consultant, women's advocate, and entrepreneurial strategist. She currently serves as the Executive Director of **R3SM, Inc.** (Recover, Rebuild, and Restore Southeast MS) a nonprofit founded following Hurricane Katrina. She has an extensive knowledge of recovery following natural disasters with a foundation in revitalization of communities, philanthropy, and economic development. Over the past four years, Mavis has provided oversight of **30** new constructions and **100+** repair projects, Recently R3SM, Inc. received recognition from the MS Business Journal as one of the "Top Nonprofits of MS" and she received acknowledgment as "Top 50 Under 40".

Mavis established **Mavis A. Creagh Consulting**, a brand that offers editing, writing, speaking, and business consultation along with *We Women Ministries,* created to empower, enrich, and elevate women from all backgrounds. Mavis founded two online series: **"Walk By Faith"** and **"Making Moves"**. In addition, she is the columnist for **BE**

Mississippi Magazine "**Making Moves in Mississippi**" Around Mississippi feature.

When she is not out building the local community, Mavis Creagh enjoys a life centered on her teenage son! Writing is yet another way she serves the world as an inspiration. She is a contributing author of the best sellers; **"Trailblazers Who Lead"**, **"Courageous Enough to Launch"**, **"B.R.E.A.T.H.E. Again** and **"Finally Free"**!

Facebook https://www.facebook.com/mavisacreagh

LinkedIn: https://www.linkedin.com/in/mavis-a-creagh

Loss Equals Life

by Rita Green

God's Plan (no Drake)

I was not one to ever dream of having children. However, God's Plan included me doing so. In 2007, I was blessed with my first child. Thirteen months later, child number two came around the bend. I made it a vow always to put them first and to do my best. The very first decision I made for my children was to allow them the opportunity of life. My son has always been here to wipe my tears, and my daughter has always been here to make me smile. They continue to do so. These little gifts have been a return on investment that I could never have expected to appreciate.

This type of thing does not happen to me.

After surviving a tumultuous relationship, I got down on my knees and prayed for God to bring me someone who would love and cherish my children and me. I met my now-husband in 2011. We started as friends, evolved into an item, and eventually became each other's spouses. The road has not always been clear, but it has been a road worth traveling. My husband had no biological children of his own. As a wife, young and able, I wanted to provide him with such. You see, I saw him as a King and wanted him to have an heir, although he saw my two little love bugs as his own. So, what did we do? We tried for a baby.

In 2012 we were successful. Baby #3 was on the way, alive and well. She had a strong heartbeat and was a welcomed surprise. I felt as if I had won the lottery. My household was about to get bigger, and my husband was about to have a biological child of his own. My children were going to have another sibling. Oh, what a wonderful thing to experience, until it was not.

It was September, and at just nine weeks, I found myself in the bathroom of my home staring down at pale pink discharge. What is this? Should I be concerned? Mother! Yes, I called my mother. She came rushing over. The look on her face told me I should be worried. I rushed to the local hospital only to be told that all was well. Go back home. You will be fine. So, I did just that. I kept my feet up and tried to take it easy. In the back of my mind, I thought I was in the clear.

Later that evening, I felt the worse pain ever. Having two previous cesareans, I had no idea how actual childbirth felt. I was having contractions. I was taken to the hospital and greeted by a vulgar and petulant individual who told his fellow nursing staff that if I could not help myself out of the wheelchair while in pain, they should roll me to the front door. Yes, while going through severe pain, both physical and emotional, I had to excuse a demon from my presence. I was then informed that I had just gone through an involuntary abortion. Those words cut me deep. I could not fathom what had happened.

The hospital staff sent me home with a prescription and a solemn "it happens to many people" remark. I was silent the entire ride home. I found the first bottle of whisky and poured myself a drink, neat. I sat on my couch for hours, just staring in space. I felt as if life had been ripped from me, and it had been. I understood the "it happens to many people" reference, but it had never happened to me. So many thoughts went through my head; "Did I move too much? Did I overdo the cleaning? Did I turn the wrong way? Did I get too stressed? Was this payback for something?" I went and stayed in a very dark place, letting little to no one in for months. Her name was Rose, and I will never forget her.

You have got to be kidding me!

I got through it, and by 2013 we were once again expecting. I was so excited. My nightmare was behind me. It was February, and while sitting at my desk at work, I started to feel a leaking sensation. I went to the bathroom. Bright red blood stared back at me from the liner of my undergarments.

I burst into a shriek as I have never heard before. I went back to my office, called my husband, and told him I was on my way to the hospital. I had some beautiful friends who followed me there to check on me. I anxiously awaited the examination results. When the nurse arrived back in the room, she asked if I was in pain. I told her I had a headache, and she said the only thing she could provide was Tylenol. "Why?" I asked. "Does that mean he is okay?" "Yes," she responded. She hooked my stomach up to a monitor, and I could hear his heartbeat. I was full of glee!

I went home and took a couple of days off to rest and keep my feet up. Then, I started having contractions again. "YOU HAVE GOT TO BE KIDDING ME!" was the first thing that came out of my mouth. I sat in my bathtub with the cold shower running down my face. I could not believe this was happening again. I rushed to my gynecologist after I went through the pain. She informed me the baby had passed. I went home, but she was wrong. I started having contractions again. I went to my previous gynecologist, who told me the baby had passed from a ruptured sack due to scar tissue and that he was still in my body. I was given an ultrasound picture of my dead baby and sent to the hospital for a few days. The doctor was going to have to remove him surgically. His name was Drew.

I was dumbfounded. I could not believe I had a second miscarriage in 6 months. I felt sterile. I felt as if I was not even a woman. Yes, I had two previous children, but why now? Why was this happening to me? I had a drink when it was all said and done. I may have even hit a blunt or two to ease the pain. Nothing worked. I was beside myself. But, in true Rita fashion, I moved on.

In November of 2014, I found out we were once again expecting. Was I excited? No. Did I anticipate a miscarriage? Yes. Guess what? I had one. Yes, my third miscarriage. This time I had a blighted ovum. The sack developed, and the baby was absorbed back into the body. By this time, I was completely numb and over it all together. March 2015, the same thing. I had a tubal pregnancy. The doctors terminated the pregnancy; loss number four. At this point, I started to tell myself that God was saving me from having a serial killer or mass murderer. This type of thinking was honestly the only way I could keep my sanity.

There is always a rainbow after the storm.

Move on to October of 2015, and yes, we found ourselves pregnant again. This time was unlike the last. I expected a miscarriage. I did not get excited. But, this time, something happened. My 101-year-old great-grandmother had a stroke. I found myself in her hospital room daily on the verge of cursing out the staff to do what they could to save her. I did not want to lose her. I had lost so much already. I begged God not to take away the main character of my childhood memories. Plus, I was pregnant. I could not bear to lose both her and the person I was carrying.

God spoke, and He took her. She had done her job well. It was time. I stood on pins and needles, wondering if the baby inside of me would suffer the same fate. Nine weeks passed, ten weeks, Eleven weeks, then twelve. I had made it past the first trimester. Then the second. Then the third. It was June 16, 2016, and I got to hold him. He made it. Oh, to hear the cries, coos, and sounds from this little person. I had been waiting to hold him for years, and he was here. He was my rainbow baby.

Twenty-one months later, my fourth and final child was born in March of 2018. I had made it through feelings of damnation, feelings of unworthiness. I crawled from the dark place of despair and continue to shine a light on my situation in the hopes that others will be encouraged. I tried to find solace in what happened; I could not. I turned to cocktails and trash tv as coping mechanisms, but that did not work. I learned to be anxious for nothing but to humbly pray about everything with a thankful heart to God (Philippians 4:6-7).

In the end, I had to realize that loss of life is inevitable as we all have an expiration date. I allowed myself to mourn. I allowed myself to feel less than. I also forgave myself the latter. I believe that God has his reasoning for things, that, more importantly, our minds are too feeble to understand what His plans include. I have learned to trust in Him with all my heart instead of leaning to my own understanding. I acknowledge Him in all my ways, and He directs my path (Proverbs 3:5-6). Never give up. Go for gold daily. If I can keep going and make it past hell, anyone can.

About Rita Green

Our world is shaped by the audacity of those born with a passion for serving humanity. As culture shifts and global demand increases, it is through the benignant lives that we are better able to see the value in others. Pioneering the importance of philanthropic necessity as a cultural norm; is the altruistic professional, Rita Green.

Rita Green is a visionary, business marketing guru, communal advocate, and the CEO and founder of Geaux Fig Co., a digital marketing and project management firm. Already a well-respected member of the business society and a proud native of Biloxi, Mississippi, Rita is often celebrated for her organic contribution to the business and economic developments of the Mississippi Gulf Coast by supporting startup companies and creating areas of opportunity for their entertainment scene. Her 15-year mark on the southeast business sector has proven to be quintessential as Rita's expertise in both consumer and business hospitality has done wonders for its various hotels and casino resorts. All of this makes her transition to personal mogulship a seamless execution.

Rita's mantra is simple: True reward is not defined by achievement; but rather measured through the lives she touches, locally, nationally, and globally.

Having high regard for education, she attended both the University of Southern Mississippi and the University of New Orleans, focusing on both, Business and Psychology. Though Rita has institutional learning to thank for her increasing business opportunities throughout her career, her altruistic nature has landed her a well-deserved seat at the table of philanthropy.

No stranger to magnanimous efforts, Rita Green has undoubtedly touched the world around her. She currently serves on the Mississippi Center for Autism and Related Developmental Disabilities and Mississippi Heroes, a nonprofit organization that highlights caregivers. This position and many others, by which Rita was a proven asset, ring clear of the commodity she truly is, not just in business but in servant leadership. Rita Green is the humble recipient of several nominations, awards, and accolades; including most recently: 100 Successful Women to Know of Gulf Coast Woman Magazine, Top Influencer Success Women's Conference, Woman of Achievement Finalist for Lighthouse Business Professional

Women Corporate Category, and Nominee for Mississippi's 50 Leading Businesswomen.

Chosen as one able to acculturate positive difference globally, Rita Green continues to inspire those in need. When she is not out helping new businesses thrive, Rita is a cherished member of her local community, a loving wife, and mother of four amazing children.

Rita Green. | Benefactress. | Leader. | Humanitarian.
Website: linktr.ee/ritagreen
Business Website: www.geauxfig.com

FEAR = Face Everything And Rise

by Paméla Michelle Tate

When most people think of Post-Traumatic Stress Syndrome, otherwise known as PTSD, they immediately think of military veterans who have fought during a war. Some people don't know that almost 50% of people diagnosed with PTSD are survivors of sexual assault. I know this because I am a survivor. I have never carried a gun onto a battlefield, but I have been fighting the trauma of being raped since I was 19 years old when the world that was supposed to be my oyster came spiraling down. For years I did as most PTSD sufferers do - I suffered silently. As a result of my silence, I sentenced myself to live in the shadows of who I formerly had been. I was depressed, withdrawn, shocked, self-medicated daily with alcohol, and I functioned on autopilot until I chose to speak up and tell what had happened to me so that I could begin my walk past hell.

I was a quiet sophomore in college, and I sang in the campus gospel choir. I decided to study psychology, and I was an active member of the Black Student Union. I had a lovely group of friends. I was extremely happy to be pledging a sorority and enjoying the unbreakable bonds of joining a sisterhood. Then in one night, my life was gone. A man stole my faith, hope, and self-esteem and took my sisters away when he brutally attacked and raped me in the college dormitory.

My mind left my cut and beaten body, and I watched myself as I laid bleeding on the floor. I kept thinking she will be coming back to check on me. She knew I was only supposed to be grabbing my book, and then I would be coming right back. The seconds and minutes felt like hours and days as I waited for my line sister to check on me. My heart was racing, tears pouring from my eyes as I heard the door to the suite open. I tried to speak as silent screams poured from my soul. I trembled and wondered if my rapist had come back, but then I heard my male roommate's husky voice shout, "Oh my God," as he grabbed my bloody face and cradled me. The shock would not allow me to answer his questions about what happened to me and who did this to me, but my body violently shook when he told me he was taking me to the hospital. He went and grabbed a blanket to cover me, and he allowed me to recover some of my dignity, but that moment ended quickly when he asked me, "Were you raped?" I sobbed for what seemed like a lifetime, forced myself to breathe, and finally nodded my head and uttered the three words that I would only say one more time in four years, "I was raped."

Things unraveled quickly after that.

He asked me, "Do you want me to call your parents?"

I was too embarrassed, so I said, "No."

He asked, "Do you want me to call your boyfriend?"

I was too heartbroken, so I said, "No."

He asked, "Who do you want me to call?"

I wept again and whispered my sister-friend's name, and I blacked out. When I woke, she was there stroking my hair, and she asked what happened. I couldn't look at her, but I mumbled, "I was raped." She tried to encourage me to call the police and go to the hospital to be examined, but I continued to refuse, so she helped me get up and shower. My roommate called another one of his frat brothers, and they stood to keep watch over me and they guarded that room for several days until I was ready to leave.

I disappeared mentally and physically. It was the end of the Fall Semester, and no one noticed, or so I thought. My sister-friend called my instructors and pretended to be my mother, and she secured all of my final assignments. I was lucky that I did not have to sit for final exams; I just had to submit final papers. The phone rang like crazy, and then I stopped hearing it. Plates of food began to pile up untouched. I couldn't eat. I developed the insomnia sleep pattern that I still have today. I began drinking to start the morning and drinking to fall asleep if I could.

The sisters from the sorority asked about me and wanted to know why I had pledged 59 days and quit so abruptly, and my choir mates were asking about me as well. The semester ended, my mother had returned from her business trip, and I finally went home. I had a six-week Winter Break, and I don't remember any of it. I remembered the comfort of my bed and being in my room and knowing life would never be the same. Time moved quickly, yet every day was long, and each day was torture. I was withdrawn, moody, angry, insecure, and always on edge. I drank, got up, ate, went to work, ate, took classes in the late afternoons and evenings so that I could avoid people, ate, did home-work, ate again, drank again, and then I tried to sleep.

Bedtime was the worst - I'd hear my rapist say, "You're beautiful," as he did things to me that no one had ever done to me before.

I hated that word. I wasn't *beautiful*. He had created an ugly mon-ster. I gained 60 pounds, and I didn't care. I never wanted to be beau-tiful again! If beauty allowed someone to justify doing something so vile, I decided I would rather be ugly and safe instead of beautiful and abused. I kept to myself; I was depressed. If I had to go somewhere and I was alone, I was very anxious, but I managed to get through it. I dated, fell in love, transferred my job to Southern California, started attending Long Beach State University, and had my first son, and then things began to erupt. All of the trauma I had experienced slowly started seeping out. I began blocking things out whenever I got overwhelmed. I kept hear-ing the word *beautiful*, and it would completely paralyze me. What I dis-covered during this time is, the mind will hide things from you until it decides it is time to deal with it.

All things that begin with a lie will ultimately become undone. I moved back to San Francisco after my son's father, and I broke up. Two weeks before my graduation, I attacked a man with food cans at the neighborhood grocery store during my final exams week because he said that my son had beautiful eyes. My local grocery checker grabbed my arm. Other employees calmed me down while the veteran I had physi-cally assaulted begged the store manager not to call the police. He didn't know what had triggered me at that moment, but it was clear to him that I was having a PTSD episode because he had PTSD. I was lucky that the store manager had mercy on me and encouraged me to get help. I believe I was banned from the store as well, but I was too mortified to go back there anyway. I couldn't go on like that anymore.

I finally told my parents and close friends that I had been raped, and I surrendered my pride and made a call to get help. I met with a therapist for two years to unravel what had happened to me and how I had allowed it to change my life. I discovered the things that triggered me. I realized that I had withdrawn from all of the women in my life because I felt like they were beautiful, and I no longer saw myself as beautiful because I had been violated. I worked hard to heal. My therapist and I explored cognitive behavior therapy, and I rewired my thoughts and actions. It was vital for me to do this so that I could accept what had happened to me and move forward. While facing my demons, God reminded me that I am *His* child, and I am so much more than any bad thing that had or would happen to me. It was time for me to learn how to walk in the sunlight again. I was no longer a victim. I had to choose to become a survivor. As a result of that, I was able to: live in my truth, learn how to love myself again, have a family, develop close friendships with women without feeling inferior to them, join the sorority that was always a part of my heart even when I was lost from their sisterhood, and most importantly I have been able to help other women in my role as a domestic abuse advocate. It wasn't easy, but it was worth it! I hope this will encourage each of you to reach out when facing challenges, ask for help so that you too can choose to face everything and rise!

About Paméla Michelle Tate

Paméla Michelle Tate is an author, community organizer, domestic violence and educational advocate. She is also the executive director of the Black Women Revolt Against Domestic Violence Resource Center.

She currently serves as the Northern California Domestic Violence Coordinator of the Zeta Phi Beta, Sorority, Inc. Delta Zeta Chapter, which she is a proud member of, and she is using the designated platform to promote, educate, resource, and to bring resolve to those burdened by the lasting effects that domestic violence leaves on its survivors.

Her transparency is well appreciated by various audiences. As a survivor, Paméla believes that it is her responsibility to champion advocacy. Through the power of her own life's story, she has become a catalyst for both local and global communities. She shares some of her story in the upcoming anthology, "My Walk Past Hell," scheduled to be released in April 2021.

Standing authentically in her purpose, Paméla has joined forces with three of her friends and formed the Black Women Revolt Against Domestic Violence Resource Center. This group is comprised of women determined to provide the various resources, tools and aid that are necessary to stand against domestic violence.

Paméla is also the author of "A GIRL'S JOURNEY: There's No Crying in Baseball," a book written to teach children and families about fortitude, integrity, gender roles and the concept of being a team player. In 2021, she released another personal piece of work, "I'll Fly Away: 31 Day Devotional for Caretakers," to offer time, space and healing for other caretakers such as herself who are caring for a parent, spouse, child, family member or friend.

When Paméla is not out advocating for others, she resides in the beautiful San Francisco Bay area. She is a beloved daughter and the mother of three children and one bonus child.

Paméla Michelle Tate
Website: www.mstatewrites.com
Facebook and Instagram: @mspamelatate

Against All Odds

by Antrinia Cardona

When I was a young girl, I remember hearing secret whispers of women getting beat on by their boyfriends and husbands. At the time, I didn't understand what I was hearing. I just shrugged it off and went back to playing childhood games, like hopscotch.

It wasn't until high school that I recall seeing a boy actually fight a girl and the weird thing was, they were dating. He whipped her in front of everyone and I felt bad for her. Afterward, I would see her in the hallway, and you could tell she was ashamed. I kept thinking to myself that it was none of my concern and that it could never be me. I became judgmental because it didn't affect me.

Soon, I started witnessing this abuse in my childhood household. Back in those days, it was taboo to talk about things like this and the old saying was always, "what happens in my house stays in my house." Man, oh, man. I had no idea that I was being groomed to inherit this very same mindset and didn't know how this old saying would almost steal my voice.

It was a fall night in 2013. I remember it was raining hard so going anywhere was out of the question. My ex-husband and I were sitting on the couch watching movies and it was kind of a boring night. Our two sons were downstairs in their bedrooms playing video games. At the time, they were about 9 and 11 years old. My ex was drinking Hennessey, and, in those days, this was a daily sport for him. I could tell that he had been dealing with something internally, but he wouldn't tell me what was going on, no matter how many times I'd asked before.

My phone made a sound notifying me of a text message. I picked it up and smiled because it was a message from one of my best friends. I was typing a response to her when he asked if the text message was from another friend. I said, "No." I thought to myself that he had some nerve questioning me when I'm not the one who got caught cheating multiple times over the last 13 years. This was also coming from the guy who ran around with nothing but single friends. He said in a stern voice, "Who is the text from then?" And then condescendingly, he said, "Oh, let me guess, it was from that dude I saw you talking to at the restaurant." I laughed to myself and thought this was so off the wall as it couldn't be further from the truth. I was so fed up with his double standards. I answered, "And if it was?" The next thing I remembered was a 6'1", 225-pound blur leaping towards me.

He jumped on top of me with a quickness. He began punching me over and over again and I tried to fight back. This time seemed very different than all the other times we fought. His face was full of anger and rage. It was as if he snapped and unleashed all of his frustrations on me. Then, he knocked me down and put me in the worst chokehold I'd ever experienced in my life. Trust me, I had endured a few of these by him. I remember wondering why he was squeezing my neck so tightly. Why hasn't he released me by now? It felt like a boa constrictor was wrapping its body tighter and tighter around my neck.

It was at that moment that I started panicking. The chokehold felt more sinister this time. It lasted far longer than any other chokehold this man had ever placed on me. At this point, I remember thinking, oh my God I can't breathe, this isn't normal. Weak and out of breath at this moment I uttered the words, "Stop, you're hurting me, I can't breathe." I began kicking my legs around and smacking him in the head in a desperate attempt to break the hold and free myself. He released one of his arms to block my hits and at this moment I screamed so loud hoping our sons or maybe even the neighbors heard me. I remember hearing one of my sons lowering the volume of his tv. He must have heard something. This prompted him to pause for a minute. A few seconds later, the volume returned to its original level. The grip tightened around my neck even more. I was so damn scared. I felt so helpless and weak. My life seemed to flash before my eyes. I thought to myself, he's going to kill me, and I will never see my sons again. This was one of my biggest fears!

Thoughts of my mother began flowing into my head. I remembered how she suffered a similar situation and didn't make it. God, I don't want to die, please help me. Suddenly, a feeling came over me, and somehow, I was able to maneuver my body in a way that broke his chokehold. Still on the ground, I scooted my body away from him. I screamed, "Get away from me, I'm not afraid of you! I will not let you do this to me!" He had a surprised look on his face. I felt different somehow. Like something fierce was awakened deep inside of me. I was scared out of my mind but enough was enough. I had to get myself out of this marriage before I repeated a horrible family cycle of abuse. This is exactly what I did.

A few months had passed, and I finally built up enough courage to pursue a divorce and put things in motion. It was different this time because I went through with it. In the past, I allowed the fear of being a single mom and worrying what others would say about me to scare me back into a bad situation. I would also think about that old saying of "what happens in my house stays in my house." Well, not this time. This was the straw that broke the camel's back, and I was determined to take my sons and move on no matter how hard it would be. I'd finally convinced myself that I deserved better.

When I think about it, this specific moment and many other episodes of mental and physical abuse I experienced have forced me to become a more resilient woman. It was not easy. I began talking to God a lot more. I asked God for the strength I needed to keep going on in life and to move past this catastrophic event. I asked him to show me my purpose. I truly felt like God led me to the sport of bodybuilding and I fell in love with it. Bodybuilding has helped me build confidence as well as physical and mental strength. I found that it gave me numerous coping mechanisms and I've relied on them as a source of healing. One day, through a conversation with God, it became clear to me that I needed to pull the cloak from myself. I needed to place myself in positions where I could help others in similar situations. But, more importantly, I needed to tell my story.

This was going to take a great deal of courage because there were only a couple of people who knew a small amount of what I was going through. I told myself that to truly help others the way I felt like I needed to, it was going to require me to be transparent, vulnerable, and to share my story. This has been extremely uncomfortable for me because I'm not used to telling people about the hell I've experienced. By sharing this story, I truly hope that it will inspire others and give them the courage they need to leave abusive situations. I want them to know that they deserve better and through God, all things are possible.

I remarried and now I have an extremely loving and supportive husband who loves me unconditionally. Experiencing this was so new for me. I'm very lucky and thankful to have him in my corner despite all the things I've been through. He has been my biggest cheerleader and has been there to encourage and boost me up when I need it most. My sons have blossomed into two intelligent, fine young men and I am very proud of them. I've tried my best to raise them the best way I know how, and they never cease to amaze me. If they ever read this, I want them to know that they helped me to survive by giving me a reason to fight through some of my darkest moments. I also have a successful career and am now a professional competitive natural bodybuilder with a couple of trophies under my belt. I now know how to defend myself and I'm not going down without a fight. I'm truly thankful that God has blessed me and continues helping me through all the trauma I've experienced. Without Him, I wouldn't have made it this far. He has helped me to gain strength and confidence and I now have a better outlook on life. My walk past this particular hell has been life-changing for me. I have bounced back and now I feel like I am better than ever!

About Antrinia Cardona

Sometimes the best way to exude uncommon strength, can be found in how we help others see, the strength they have, within themselves. Committed to showing people that exact value, is the compassionate advocate, Antrinia Cardona.

Antrinia Cardona is an author, athletic exponent, and a certified Master Resilience Trainer, with a passion for Sexual Assault Victim and Domestic Violence Advocacy. Serving as an active-duty Chief Master Sergeant in the Air Force for 23 years, Antrinia uses her testimonial platform, of having survived domestic abuse, since early childhood; as a transformational coaching experience, she now infuses in her program, to help many victims, confront their abuse and abusers; so that they can live, victoriously. Her prolific message of advocacy, coupled with her profession, has helped many service members overcome their traumatic pasts; an intention Antrinia values more than anything.

Antrinia's Mantra is simple: she was born to empower people by sharing her story as a domestic violence survivor. She wants

them to be able to accept their struggles, and use them as fuel, to become more resilient in life.

Though inspired by advocacy overall, Antrinia pairs her philanthropic gesture, with a regard for higher learning. Antrinia is a member of the Delta Mu Delta Business Honor Society and has acquired an Associate in Applied Science of Maintenance Production Management, in 2007; a Bachelor of Business Administration, with a concentration in Information Technology, in 2013, and a Master of Business Administration, with a concentration in Accounting; in 2017.

Antrinia has touched many lives through the ethics she practices as a professional bodybuilder and resilient trainer. Her greatest joy has been in helping women to educate, empower, and boost their confidence levels; in order to restore their inner and outer strength.

When Antrinia is not out stewarding others into their best lives, she is a cherished asset of her communal body and a loving member of her family and friendship circles.

Antrinia Cardona. | Leader. | Advocate. | Survivor.
Email address: antriniacardonacoaching@gmail.com
Facebook: Antrinia Cardona Coaching

calm, firm voice, "JoAnne, it's not you! It's him. It was me. "What do you mean?" I asked. His response was, "He is insecure and sees you as a threat. When we were together, I wanted to break you." Why?' I asked. He said, "Because you were always right. We talked about everything, made all the decisions together, yet I wanted to do what I wanted. Whenever I did it my way, it turned out bad, and I ended up going back to what we had decided. That made me angry, and yet you never said, "I told you so." This guy is trying to do the same thing". You are strong! Your strength is a threat to any man who is unsure of himself and weak. When I started messing up, your strength is what angered me. That is why I wanted to break you. This man wants to do the same." I told him, "You almost did." He responded, "I couldn't see it." He then apologized again for everything, and I replied, "All is forgiven, and thank you for explaining why things happened because I always blamed myself, as I am doing now." He said, "It is not you." Suddenly I felt a sense of peace between us. After that conversation, James and I would talk at least once a week.

In April of 2017, after he could no longer bear the pain in his right shoulder, James sought medical attention. We knew the pain had to be unbearable because James hated needles and doctors. James's diagnosis was COPD and Stage 4 Lung Cancer, and we had three years with him. At this time, he had three grown children and one minor. I got a call from my daughter explaining that her father was writing his last will. He asked if I would be the legal guardian for his then five-year-old daughter. I happily agreed, thinking nothing was going to happen. His physician unexpectedly called us on a Monday to explain how things had taken a turn for the worst. Three years suddenly turned into three days. We arrived in Florida on Wednesday evening. As I stood next to his bedside watching him. I noticed he was alert, and his breathing was labored. I took his hand, he looked at me and smiled. I touched his once coarse hair and noticed it soft and curly. His complexion was as flawless as the day we met. His once rough, callused, hard-working hands were now soft and smooth. It did not feel like he was transitioning.

My daughter spent the night at his bedside. I arrived early Thursday morning to relieve and allow her a chance to shower and change clothes. While sitting in James' room, listening to the shower run, I saw the large letters DNR written on the bulletin board and thought nothing of it. I called his name and held his hand. He opened his eyes and smiled again. That was the moment years of pain and abuse honestly became the past. In a matter of seconds, his labored breathing suddenly turned normal. I knew this was not a good sign. My mom walked in, and I asked her to get the nurse. The nurse confirmed he was transitioning, and he did. Thankfully, he was not alone. It was all so surreal!

We knew we had to move forward without James. I felt as if God was saying to me, "You say you forgive him. Now prove it!" Our children were not mentally or emotionally prepared to handle the final arrangements for their father at the time. I said, "Ok, Lord, what am I supposed to do?" I put aside my grieving and stepped in to help plan and arrange the memorial service in Florida and funeral arrangements in Virginia. When it was all said and done, I came home with a beautiful five-year-old girl as "My Gift of Forgiveness." Tyler Perry said it best, "It's not an easy journey, to get to a place where you forgive people. But is such a powerful place because it frees you."

About Dr. JoAnne Hayes

Legacy is achieved when brave individuals decide to make life a learning hub for the next generation of women. Leading by example is the dynamic professional, Dr. JoAnne Hayes.

Dr. JoAnne Hayes is an author, servant leader, business expert, and an educational advocate, with a passion for people. Having strong professional expertise in the realms of business administration, legal acumen, and servant leadership. Dr. Hayes has a heart for overall literacy and the implementation of educational support needed in society; to see others thrive.

Dr. JoAnne's mantra is simple: She believes in education at any age; for everyone. Dr. Hayes believes that we should strive to learn something new every day, without ceasing.

Dr. JoAnne's appreciation for higher learning is apparent. She received her Bachelor of Science degree from North Carolina A&T

State University. Her most recent success was attaining her Doctorate in Business Administration with a concentration in Human Resource Management from Walden University. As an advocate for survivors of domestic violence, and she is a speaker of the Survivor's Council for the local women's shelter. Being a volunteer tutor and a youth mentor in her faith-based community is near and dear to her heart.

Dr. JoAnne Hayes is inspired by a will to serve others and the achievements attained throughout her educational journey. She continues to be one who helps others sojourn that same legendary experience. Her desire is to become the best coach, teacher, and inspiration to women of all ages so that they too can experience the best of life *while learning.*

When Dr. JoAnne is not teaching the world new things, she is into crafting, sewing, and reading. She is a beloved member of her community, a mother to three children, and G*lam-ma* to one incredible granddaughter.

Dr. JoAnne Hayes. | Leader. | Educator. | Legacy-Builder.
Facebook: Dr-JoAnne White Hayes
Instagram: drjoannehayes

The Sound of Silence

by Christina Warner

I thought I had spent more than my fair share of time walking through Hell. I had gotten so used to the heat my walk no longer seemed treacherous, more like a rite of passage. SI was surviving every day at the hands of a molester who couldn't get enough of touching me. I endured his wandering hands regularly, thinking I was protecting my loved ones. Looking back, I realize that was such a burden for a child to carry – … protecting others. I should have been the one protected. Little did I know his wondering wandering hands, gazing eyes, and sadistic mindset was just the entry fee into the next level of Hell.

Chest pounding, palms sweaty, and mouth dry, I called my mother. I didn't have the best relationship with her, but something compelled me to call. The phone seemed to ring 1000 times before she picked up. I remember each heartbeat ringing loudly in my ear and pounding my chest before I murmured "I'm pregnant," followed by the longest, most defining deafening silence.

I wanted her to give me words of encouragement, but my mind knew her words would be anything but. She finally said, "Why would you do that? Now you're not gonna be anything. You're not gonna go to college. Your life is over. Why?"

I hung up. Leaning against the wall, I slid down on the floor, thinking I have never felt this alone. The silence in the house and aching in my heart rang so loud I couldn't hear anything, like a bomb exploding, sucking all the sound from around me. I had nothing and no one. Alone. Scared. Pregnant. Those three words repeated in my head over and over again. I joined the military to escape Hell, 500 plus miles away, and I still wasn't free. Alone. Scared. Pregnant and the punching bag for the father of my children. Trapped again by the hands of another man, from sexual touches to punches, slaps, and daily degrading. My first walk through Hell seemed like a Sunday stroll in comparison.

As I sat on the floor, I wondered, "Is this supposed to be my life? I guess this is my life." I sat there alone in the dark for hours. I didn't move, and I contemplated, "Why am I here? Why should I live?"

I didn't want to live. To be alone with so many people around you. I wore a smile on my face every day and was dead on the inside. I got into some trouble at work, so I was discounted and overlooked. I didn't have anyone to talk to, no friends. I was embarrassed and ashamed. Hurting and wishing someone would ask, "How are you?" and mean it. I didn't want the words "How are you?" to not just be a reactionary phrase after the words, "Good morning." For someone to mean it…sadly no one asked.

In my head, there was a girl screaming, "How! How!! Hoooow!!" I was destined to be at the bottom; there was no happiness or love for me. My mother was right. I cried silent tears and screamed with no sound from a place of deep pain, so deep a punch to the face or cracked rib was nothing compared to the aching loneliness I felt. I was paralyzed mentally and physically. I sat for hours in denial about being my almost four months' pregnancy, with twins. I had been hit so many times, slammed against the wall, spit at, choked, and tormented that I was un-sure how I could even be pregnant. I don't know how the twins sur-vived. God was protecting them because I couldn't.

A month went by, and it became apparent that everything was my fault. I could not say or do anything right. There was nothing good in his life and I needed to pay for that. Each day I got up checked myself for marks, bruises, any telling signs, put on a masked smile for work to come "home" to his terror. When I walked in the door of my home my body was checked to see if I had slept with someone while I was at work. I had to take my clothes off at the door and get checked. Nothing could look different from when I left. It was my routine Hell. Walking in the house and closing the front door sucked all the life out of me, like a penitentiary door separates an inmate from freedom. I was too trapped. There were no nights of peace. The more we fought, the more I thought, "It's ok… it's ok to die now. You don't have to suffer anymore. This isn't love."

I would lay praying to just die. As he hit me, I was every dirty and demeaning name a person could be. I became mentally and physically numb to everything around me. I could take a punch like a boxer easily. At times, I would giggle, thinking, "…That's all you got?", when I felt his strike. The words alone, scared, pregnant played over and over as I zoned out from the pain regularly.

One sound I could hear all the time was my duplex neighbors. If I heard them casually throughout the day, I know they could hear my screams for help, m. My cries of pain. I would scream to the top of my lungs, hoping someone would help. I remember the loud thud when my head was rammed into the wall, I know they heard me heard the wall break. They heard my screams and my cries for help; no one ever called the police.

Alone. Scared. Pregnant. Forgotten. Replayed in my head. Over and over, I felt alone, and there is no feeling in the world like having no way out. A—all these people around me and no help. Duplex neighbors a large cul-de-sac of fellow military members and stay-at-home moms who walked by my house every day. It pained me to see other people happy and living a beautiful life and every day as I suffered and drowned in my silence. One thing I knew for sure I could do, or control was not bringing the babies in my belly into the Hell I lived in. I tried on two occasions to have an abortion but couldn't do so. I felt even more like a failure; I couldn't protect my babies. I was going to give birth and bring children into a world of Hell. They did not deserve it and further solidified my understanding that I didn't need to be here, let alone be there their mother. I will be a horrible mother for bringing them into a world of so much pain and fighting. As my stomach grew, I wondered, "Do they feel it when I get hit? Do, they know the emptiness I feel? All my babies deserved was to be loved and feel wanted and I didn't want them birthed into my Hell. I hated myself.

I hated myself until the day my abuser took a big master lock and threw it at my stomach. I hadn't felt physical pain like that. I fell, and I finally got angry!!! I got my fight back and said no more. It was justified if I got an abortion. I could have dealt with that because I controlled the situation. He did not get the option to take my babies away from me. From then on, every fight I fought back. He punched and kicked, and so did I. I fought to live, be free and protect my babies.

Another month went by, and I was about six months pregnant when he locked me outside of the house for hours. I didn't have anywhere to go to the bathroom, no food and water. I tried everything to get back in. We lived in this little cul-de-sac. All my neighbors walked by me said, "hello," but never offered to help. No one ever offered me anything. Some walked past by three or 4 four times throughout the day. Finally, in desperation, I told him, "I'm sorry I'm always messing things up; if you let me in, I'll behave."

He came to the door smiling, and I remember him cracking the door just slightly. As his face was peeping through the door, I used every ounce of strength I had and pushed the door so hard – I wanted to break his face. I wanted him to feel a smidgen of what I felt every day. He fell to the floor, and I was so tired and so hungry I just stepped right over him, and I went to the refrigerator and ate everything I could. It was then that I knew I wanted to live. I didn't want this life. I had to figure a way out. What were my options? This wasn't the life for me. Everything changed.

Finally, I left with nothing but the clothes on my back and the babies in their car seat. I was too young in my career to know there was plenty more the military could have done to help me. I didn't know the rules. I asked for help, and in every direction, I turned, there was no one to help me. I had no money. I couldn't afford a divorce. The road from there wasn't easy. I lost my children to foster care. Though I didn't have my children, God sent them an Angel to love and care for them. She was the best thing that could have happened to them. I am forever grateful for every blessing she provided.

While serving on active duty, I worked two jobs went to anger management classes, parenting classes, and paid the state fees for having kids in foster care while my abuser walked around with no obligations. I was running out of leave/vacation at the military job. Time, I needed to sleep because I was exhausted trying to meet the demands of the state and the military state and the military's demands. I had to prove to the military, the court, and myself I could do it. Meaning I could serve and still be a mother at the same time.

I stepped into my freedom. Despite my past, I was able to come out of Hell with a fierce walk, a determined mind, and a grateful soul. I made Staff Sergeant the first time I tested and got my divorce paid in full by a domestic violence attorney. I stood on my own feet, free, with a real smile and weights of terror lifted. I got away from both of my abusers. I survived my stepdad, and I escaped my ex-husband. My two beautiful girls and I were finally able to get away out and live. I thank God I don't look like what I've been through.

About Christina Warner

The defining principles of Organizational Leadership are not established through the eloquence of intelligence and diplomacy alone, but rather from driven leaders, surrendered to the processes of character development, wisdom, and innate advocacy. Unyieldingly devoted to the sum of all these traits; is the compassionate leader, Christina Warner.

Christina Warner is an author, advocate, business guru, and a Chief Master Sergeant, with a high propensity for helping clients, establish economy around entrepreneurial ventures. Currently servicing military personnel and many more; as the enlisted functional manager for Air Force Combat Command. She is also the principal advisor to the Senior Contracting Official, advising others on contracting policies affecting enlisted personnel. Christina proudly serves 14 bases on contracting and enlisted matters regarding quality of life, morale, health, and welfare of the contracting workforce. While hosting an impressive working reliability for many; it is her commitment in helping others, realize their truest potential, that motivates her outstanding delivery.

Christina's Mantra is simple: Tackle complex and layered situations with unparalleled competence and concrete commitment.

Christina Warner backs a tenacious work ethic with a regard for higher learning; as she has successfully completed her bachelor's in computer science; Associates Degrees in both, Business Administration/Logistics Management and Contracts Management. Christina obtained honors as an Instructor of Technology and Military Science, in 2005. She is certified in top tier acquisitions such as: Contracting Level III, Defense Acquisition University; Professional Managers, Instructional Systems Development, Occupational Instruction, and many more.

Today, Christina Warner is one of the top 1% of leaders, accomplishing more than 17 years of experience-based leadership, coaching and team building; in the world's largest military. An accomplishment that while praised greatly; came off the back of trauma, dedication, and an undying will to persevere; despite all odds. Christina inspires many, advising them all that she took what was meant to destroy her and transformed it; in order to be a guiding lamp for others suffering, through tough times. She looks to be a consistent inspiration to all; especially women, reminding them of their greatness and that they can survive and be successful, indefinitely. She is also the founder and CEO of She Persevered, LLC and Consulting with Joy. The mission of She Persevered is to help people reach their highest potential, while Consulting with Joy's mission is to help others business dreams become a reality.

When Christina is not our advocating for female entrepreneurs, she is an important figure to her communal body, and a beloved mother of four, sister of two siblings, and dedicated friend to her friendship circles.

Christina Warner. | Leader. | Guru. | Advocate.
Business e-mail: Sheperseveredllc@gmail.com

Devil at My Door

by Ashira Windsor

There I was, nine months pregnant with my baby boy, riding shotgun on the passenger side seat of my boyfriend's black Honda Accord. He was driving no less than 100mph, barreling towards a moving train on the track, telling me that he was going to kill us both. At that moment, my heart was racing; I was thinking, "What have I done to myself?" Quietly, praying to God, promising to him that I would do better if he delivered me. There is no way I could have known that a night of playing chicken with the train would lead to one of the most hellacious moments of my life. It dawned on me at this moment that I did not love this man, and there was no way that he could love me, but I felt stuck with no way out. I knew that I would have to be strategic in my escape from this man, and it would take me at least another two years to break free of him but not before he tried to end my life.

Fast forward to the day after my near miss with tons of quickly moving steel; I was lying nine months pregnant on the floor in someone else's apartment trying to sleep because I'd argued with my family when I experienced what I could only explain as the worst pain I'd ever felt in my life. I'd never felt a contraction before, but I knew that it wasn't supposed to feel like this. I woke my boyfriend, who was also sleeping on the same floor, and told him that I was in tremendous pain and needed to go to the hospital. By this time, I was pouring sweat and screaming in pain. It was at this time that I knew that I needed him to speed as quickly to the hospital as he'd sped towards that moving train the night before. Little did I know that September 29, 1995, was about to change my life forever.

Upon arrival at the hospital, I was drenched in sweat and unable to walk. As the hospital staff pulled me out of the car, they started calling codes, and I was taken into a room where medical staff instantly started looking for my baby boy's heartbeat. By this time, my mother had found her way to my side. A short time later, the doctor would walk in and share the devastating news that my baby's heart was no longer beating. I was in utter shock and confusion, refusing to accept the prognosis, praying against everything that a miracle would take place. Soon after, I was rushed to surgery as I'd sustained internal injuries and was losing blood fast. My mother was allowed to stand by my side as they made the cut to remove my baby boy. In a state of denial, I prayed like I'd never prayed for anything before, that my son would emerge from my womb alive and screaming, but that was not the case. I was handed a beautiful, perfectly formed 7lb 13oz baby boy, making it even harder to accept that he was not breathing. At that moment, I felt pain and anger like no other. I felt robbed and like I'd been forsaken by all, including God. I'd dealt and put up with nine months of abuse not only from my boyfriend but his family, who thought I was unworthy of their morally bankrupt brother, all to end up with nothing to show for it.

I would wake up the next morning in intensive care, only to understand that I had been within an inch of losing my life due to a placental abruption. Was I dreaming? I had to be dreaming! There was no way that my first and only son was never allowed to take one breath on this earth! I instantly began asking the staff for my baby boy, hoping against hope that this was all a bad dream. They complied.

A nurse would soon return with my beautiful baby boy, who'd been dressed in the cutest blue clothing. Excited, I reached for my baby boy thinking, "I knew he wasn't dead," but to my shock, when they placed him in my arms, it was apparent that he wasn't living. He was cold as ice and void of all movement, and my heart broke again. I asked the nurse why he'd been dressed and groomed; she explained that they wanted to allow me to spend as much time with him as I could. They would bring him to me to hold anytime I requested until he was no longer there. I would go on to spend several additional days in intensive care. I would sleep, wake up and relive the nightmare of my loss again. It felt like I'd awakened from a nightmare only to find out there was no nightmare, but only the stinging reality of my loss. This was the darkest moment of my young life.

It was finally time for me to be released from the hospital and attend my son's funeral service. His funeral had been planned and paid for by the very people who'd demeaned me and denied my baby the entire nine months I carried him, my boyfriend's family. They could no longer deny him because he was born the spitting image of them. I made it through the funeral and burial, by the grace of God, and remember saying to myself, "there is no way I could ever feel this low in life again." Alas, life would go on to prove me wrong; this was only the beginning of "my walk past hell." It would take me an additional two years to walk past my hell and on to victory.

Three months after the loss of my son, I would learn that I was pregnant again, with whom I now consider my rainbow baby. I would be lying to myself if I didn't admit that I'd often had thoughts of how I'd allowed myself to get pregnant again, for the man that'd abused me so many times mentally and physically. As I think back on it, I'm not sure if I had control or a choice. In spite of my feelings of uncertainty, the pain I felt from the loss of losing my son was soothed by being allowed to carry life inside of me again. Shockingly, my boyfriend didn't lay a hand on me the entire nine months of my pregnancy, though he never said why; I knew he felt guilt about the loss of his son based on abuse at his hands. As a result, I was able to deliver a healthy and beautiful baby girl on September 30, 1996, almost exactly one year after the loss of my son.

It would only take two weeks after the birth of my daughter, though, for my boyfriend to unleash all nine months of his pinned-up anger and frustration onto me. This anger led to me being dragged down a flight of stairs in my pajamas while still healing from a cesarean section and being thrown out of my home for several days with no access to my daughter. It was at this time that I decided enough was enough! I wasn't going to take his abuse any longer. If I wanted something better, I had to do something different. I decided that I first had to learn how to love and build myself up so I would have the strength necessary to break free and overcome my situation. As a result, in 1997, I enrolled in a local vocational school not only as an escape from the daily abuse but as a way to start building myself up again.

During my time at the vocational school, my confidence was being restored. I started to remember who I was as a person and gained the courage to start taking steps to leave my abusive relationship. It would ultimately take my boyfriend stomping and breaking the fingers on my right hand, coupled with one of my classmates being killed in the same week after attempting to escape her abusive relationship, to give me the courage needed to end the relationship with my abuser.

It's 1998, and as a newly freed woman, I would get my first official job at Louisiana State University, which allowed me to afford my first place living on my own. Things with my ex-boyfriend had become relatively quiet, and life began to feel normal for me again. BAM, BAM, BAM, BAM! There was a loud banging at the door of my apartment. Evidently, my ex had learned that I was dating again and decided to intervene. After I didn't answer the door, my ex proceeded to kick the door in which ultimately resulted in one of the most terrifying moments in my life. I tried to run to a neighbor's home to get help, but there was no answer. I ran to the back of the building where my ex-boyfriend caught me and tried to make good on the many threats he'd issued over the years to take my life.

As the first punch hit my face and I fell to the ground, my life flashed before my eyes; I knew that I was about to die, but once again, I asked God to keep me as this person whom I'd bared two children for stomped my face until something or someone scared him away. By the grace of God, I didn't lose consciousness and was able to stumble my way onto the roadway in an effort to get help. The guy that I'd been dating was searching for me at the same time, found me, loaded me into his truck, and took me to my mother's home. I was rushed to the hospital, where I would later find out that every bone in the left side of my face had been broken and that my left eye had been knocked in. My injuries resulted in a 10-hour surgery and me being told that I would never see fully out of my left eye, nor would I feel anything on the left side of my face again. At this very moment, I decided that the devil would not win, nor would I accept the prognosis of the doctor. Once I felt good enough, I attended a local church where whom I considered my spiritual father was a visiting pastor from California, the moment I, a stranger, walked through the door, the congregation approached, laid hands on me, and began to pray, there was a healing in the cards for me.

The fear I once felt about my ex-boyfriend taking my life was gone as he'd done his worst. It was at this time; I knew that I was truly free. My face and my eye would fully heal, and I would go on to receive four college degrees, marry the love of my life, and rear beautiful and conscientious children. I'd made it through "My Walk Past Hell," and I, with the help of God, had defeated the devil at my door, and he'd been sent back to the pits of hell where whence he came. I was no longer a "victim" I was "victorious."

About Ashira Windsor

We live in a world encompassed by a deep need for personal understanding, spiritual growth, and change. Determined to meet that need, one person at a time; is the compassionate professional, Ashira Windsor.

Ashira Windsor is an author, advocate, clinical social worker, and the Owner and Lead Therapist of Catalyst Counseling and Therapy Services; a multi-dimensional practice, committed to the wellness of individuals, families, and the community; through the necessary methods of prevention, intervention, treatment and education. While having established an outstanding career as both, a licensed and certified social worker; in the states of California and Mississippi, Ashira Windsor is thoroughly committed to the breakthrough of both, clients and professionals; through the specialty, of Catalyst Counseling and Therapy Services. Adjoining her purpose for healing others, with the establishment of facilitating more space for professionals, called to the same standard;

Catalyst Counseling and Therapy Services is also a breeding ground for Social Workers in training, and doubles as an internship site for universities around the country.

Ashira, most recent accomplishment is co-founding "Bridging the Gap Transitional Age Youth Program," a nonprofit organization in 2020. Bridging the Gap's ultimate goal is to be the runway that gives teens aging out of the foster care system the momentum they need to be successful in life.

Ashira's Mantra is simple: She has a genuine love for her profession, and the opportunities it allows her to help others.

Ashira pairs the principle of her practice with a regard for higher learning, as she has received her Bachelor of Social Work from Norfolk State University, Norfolk, VA., and her Master of Social Work from the University of Southern California, Los Angeles, CA. She is backed by more than 10 years in her field and licensed in both Mississippi and California.

Ashira combines the ethics of her professionalism, with an unyielding love for philanthropic efforts. Through her life's work, she has been able to provide an extensive volunteer experience; with the provision of case management, counseling, and therapy to individuals struggling with mental illness, behavioral health issues, familial issues, homelessness and co-occurring disorders. Her trusted reliability has made her the keynote speaker at several Social Work Conferences, and a guest speaker at many women's empowerment conferences, on the Gulf Coast.

When Ashira is not out advocating for the world at large, she enjoys reading, traveling, aquariums and spending time with close family and friends. She remains a strong asset to her communal body; a loving wife to an active-duty Navy Seabee, and a loving mother to five children.

Ashira Windsor. | Advocate. | Leader. | Philanthropist.
Business website: www.catalystcounselingandtherapy.com
E-mail: ashira.windsor@yahoo.com

Believe Warriors Are Born To Conquer, Soar, Slay, And Breakthrough All Hell! Dreams vs. Nightmares

by Dr. Nichole Peters

*A*ll my life, I was always the type that had dreams versus night-mares. Ever since I was a child, the enemy wanted me in his hell camp of brimstones and fire. He wanted me to be part of his darkness to keep me blinded, living a life of hell with no return. He banked on me, fearing him instead of God. He knew Father God wanted me as one of His warriors. He knew at an early age my relation-ship with The Lord was so dope. He hated the fact that Father God was training and equipping me in His spiritual camp so I could conquer every battle I was faced with, soar and rise above every failure to slay every demonic darkness that came my way. Every traumatic experi-enced I went through, I knew Father God was there with me, walking me through the fire.

Some nights after I prayed, my G'ro (my grandma) would tuck me in and pray again. Why? Because I would have some very strong visions and dreams where Father God would show me how I would help other people get out of bondage. One Christmas, my dad, drove to New Orleans to purchase a Wonder Woman costume for me. You couldn't tell me I didn't have powers like Wonder Woman and run fast like Bionic Woman. When I was young, my dreams and visions were extremely strong. I'd act them out in reality. Living in the projects, peo-ple always needed help.

"Grandma, I'm going to help the poor, so folks don't have to live off assistance, so people can stop saying they're lazy cause they live in the PJs. In my dreams, helping so many who were being abused, stressed, downtrodden, and didn't want to live anymore was powerful. Grandma, just like when those mean students try to bully my friends, I was there to save them. I'm not scared to face bullies head-on. When my friends in the projects were hungry, I would fix them peanut butter sandwiches and juice so they wouldn't be hungry." My grandma was my biggest cheerleader; she would say, "That's my grandbaby right there. Let God continue to use you. Many grown people don't even have visions. Here you are at seven years old, talking about how GOD continues to come to you. Let God equip you for every battle. This way, you will always be ready for any darkness that you face."

You see, not only did I have visions and dreams, but I also used to have extremely dark demonic nightmares that use to try to suck the life out of me. These nightmares used to seem so real that some nights I stayed up scared to go to sleep because the enemy haunted me like a lion ready for his next meal. In my nightmares, this dark person used to tell me to kill myself and just die. Nobody loves you. You'll never be anything. You're useless on this earth. I need you in my camp; I used to have to battle this demonic monster severely in my nightmares. For some odd reason, my mindset was on his hit list. If the enemy can take your mindset, he has got you. Stealing your mind, killing your dreams, and destroying your life is his #1 goal. I used to scream out while battling my nightmares, "get off me, monster. "Granny would tell me to open my mouth and pray. Use your sword; the power of your tongue will make the enemy flee like never before. This was my game changer for everything I faced from here on out!

Here are my five ways you can walk past hell!

1. **PRAYER IS THE KEY! I** was caught up in an abusive and controlling relationship that almost cost me my life twice. I was struck in my head three times with a gun. The steel from that gun felt so very cold. I still have thoughts of how frozen my mind went at that very moment. While my EX beat me, kicked me, and did some things that should not be done to any woman, I watched my life flash right before my eyes. To stop him from

wounding me, all I could do was pray and plead to God to stop this mad man from abusing me. He was literally trying to beat my brains out (just what the enemy wanted ever since I was a child). The enemy would go through people you love to cause harm to you. It was so unfortunate he used the man I was sharing the same heart, bed, and love to attack me in such a vicious way. There was one scripture that came to mind. Mark 11:24 "Therefore I say unto you, what things soever ye desire, when ye pray, believe that ye receive them, and ye shall have them." I believed that if I kept praying to God for him to stop beating me, he would. I had to fight and have sex with him too. I believed only God could stop him. Evil had taken control of his body. He completely lost it; He didn't look or smell the same. His eyes kept going up as if he was possessed. Trust me when I say I was in the battle of my life. Only the power of prayer kept me alive. Even now, I suffer from migraine headaches, short-term memory loss, declined motor and cognitive skills. I had to go through therapy for many reasons. But I am here; I am still more than a conqueror. Why? Because I choose not to give up, instead I choose to win this war. Stand up against abuse. I choose to be an overcomer in such a major way by standing my ground mentally and morally. Father God heard my cry!

2. **SOAR!** Now is the time for you to Soar, which is to fly. Rise high above while maintaining height in the air. When you soar, you become laser focused. Your whole mindset is on rising above anything that's in your way. I decided not to let what happen to me take my power away from me, but instead, I started my own organization called Women of Love, Power, and Respect. I traveled around coaching other women to boldly find true love and never live with abuse. My organization has over 58,000 followers and is still growing. Soar and know GOD is with you. "But they who wait for the Lord shall renew their strength; they shall mount up with wings like eagles; they shall run and not be weary; they shall walk and not faint." Isiah 40:31

Eagles soar, and so can you. Fly above abuse!

3. **I MEAN YOU BETTER SLAY!** Now is the time for you to walk with your head up and not down. Walk with complete SLAY authority. Trample over the enemy with every step. Slay in every aspect of your life. Physically, Mentally, Emotionally, Financially, and Spiritually. When you are a demon slayer, the enemy gets a huge black eye. "I see you working, GOD." Read Psalms 35.

4. **NOW IS YOUR TIME TO WALK PAST HELL!** I lived in hell on this earth, running from God's purpose for my life. Just like Jonah was in the belly of the whale going through hell. I was around here on this living earth going through one hell after another. I remember so many people turning on me because of the color of my dark skin. I remember others looking down on me because I was raised in the projects. I remember being treated so unfairly by my own teacher because I wasn't one of her top students. I was even stabbed in the back multiple times by some family and so called friends who I've lent the shirt off my back. And what is worse is that my health failed me. I was on 14 medications; my health was so bad, I had to file for total disability. I thought it was over for me. Being highly medicated, I could hardly function. My kids watched me as I struggled with holding my fork to feed myself. I was seeing over seven different specialists, Rheumatologist, Urologist, and Neurologist, to name a few. I was literally ready to die from the pain. Watching my body get weaker and sicker was a battle of hell. Only GOD could snatch me out of that hell. Only GOD could say, my child, you've borne enough, only GOD's voice was saying rise above my daughter and fight! Jeremiah 30:17 says, "I will restore your health, and I will heal your wounds." I read this scripture about 107 times daily. This scripture I'd pass out from praying without ceasing. Now I am on four medications. Have faith that God will heal you. Believe!

5. **BREAKTHROUGH AND WALK STRAIGHT INTO YOUR DESTINY** Now is time for you to break every barrier that in your way. Surround yourself with light, with people who want to

see you grow and shine. Breakthrough by staying resilient through every chaotic experience that tries to take you down; You stay in total power by being equipped 365 days a year. Always have your war clothes on. Be prepared for evil principalities and battles of the unknown so you will be ready to obliterate his plans in the worse way. In order to get to your destiny, you must be a warrior in the mind. Always remember you are never fighting alone. God is on the battlefield with you. Trust Him and just stand on Exodus 14:14.

Here is a walk past hell challenge for you. Go to your favorite mirror and repeat, I am enough, loved, and will live in peace and not hell. I declare and decree from this day forward every chain of hell is broken off me and shattered into the pits of hell. I am now free from my past, blessed and highly favored, and am now walking in the authority of a ready warrior! I BELIEVE!

About Dr. Nichole Peters

Dr. Nichole Peters is a professional certified life coach, media mogul, international motivational speaker, executive producer, journalist, publisher and #1 best-selling award-winning author of many books. In 2020, Dr. Nichole received her PHD in Leadership and Biblical Studies. In 2019, she received two honorary doctorates in Christian education and counseling. She is the CEO/Founder of Believe In Your Dreams Academy, publishing and television.

Dr. Nichole loves reaching back coaching Women and youth who suffered from traumatic experiences to become Believe Warriors by snatching back their power of self-love through Supernatural PRAYERS, natural healing/wellness retreats and empowerment conferences. She is a die-hard advocate for domestic violence survivors. Many Surviving Believe Warriors calls her "The Breakthrough Catalyst" of this hurting era that we live in now.

The passion and the power in her voice when she speaks is reaching millions of wounded souls from all around the world. Over the past decade, Dr. Nichole garnered a social media following of over 80,000 with an international reach of 4.2 million. She is also the Founder/CEO of Women of Love, Power and Respect. She stands bold as a lion to deliver many powerful messages of hope and healing to all the hurting muted souls to break every chain that is holding them back. By always snatching back their healing power to believe in themselves, plus others in every aspect of their lives, and to always live off real love and not abuse. Come on my sisters we got this!

Text: Want to learn more about Dr. Nichole text DREAMS to 64600.

Facebook: www.Facebook.com/luvpowerrespect

The Comeback Kid

by Paula Farve

I t was a cold Southern Damp December day; as I stood in front of the old gas heater on the wall, I saw a TV commercial, Fresh and Fancy. As the commercial continued to play, I quickly ran across the cold wooden paste wax floor to the kitchen where Mamma was cooking. I danced around singing along with the commercial, "Fresh and Fancy!"

I asked my Mamma, "can I please add this to my wish list?"

She said I had to go and ask my Daddy. I ran to my room and got the Old Sears and Roebuck Christmas Catalogue. I had marked the pages and folded them as I always did. I ran down the hallway past the gun rack from the ceiling to the floor, and my heart was beating fast. I knocked on my Dad's door, and I told him that mom said I had to ask him for what I wanted on my wish list.

He said, "Oh, you want to be a big girl asking for makeup?" As the words left his lips, I knew something was not right.

He said, "I will get it if you show me if your hair is red down there like it is on your head."

I cried and ran to tell my mom. I heard yelling, and my mom told my dad that we would leave, and she would kill him if he touched her daughter.

The advances progressed and became more aggressive, and the touching began. He would jingle his change, and that was his sign for me to come. Until this day, I go into a trance when men jingle change in their pocket. That's why I have so much pride; I would never ask a man for money.

I ran away because I figured my mom had 13 other kids, I felt that she would have a husband, and my siblings needed a Dad. My mom did not leave with me as she said. So, I just ran with my niece to the police station. I realized late in life that I ran from my problems.

I went on to live with some relatives. One day I was taking a shower, and I was literally scrubbing my skin raw because I felt filthy. One day one of my relatives caught me scrubbing and starting chanting, "Chester, Chester, the child molester," and the others joined in. I stood there, naked and humiliated. That was the first time I attempted suicide. I could not take the humiliation; I felt like everyone knew my shame. I did not want to die; this was merely a cry for help.

I was placed in foster care, and almost every home I went to, the father would make advances toward me, or the mother would seem to be jealous of me. I had very long hair, so they would do things like simply cut my hair off. For years I would try and hide my curvaceous body. The foster parents would also use the money for clothing for their other kids instead of me. No one wanted to adopt a 15-year-old.

I went on to be married three times, all ending in divorce, all with abusive behavior mentally or physically. Because that is all I knew. I would also instigate fights if I was not getting the attention I wanted. It had merely become a pattern.

I had gotten into a fight with one of my husbands and ripped his tank top. He would take that very tank top and choke me with it, then would hang it over the headboard. I threw it away on numerous occasions, but it would eventually be back on the headboard.

The straw that broke the camel's back, I was attacked on my birthday in front of my ex's family. I did not want my family to visit because I knew that would pick up on at least the verbal abuse. He had grabbed me around my neck; I had on a wire necklace that had sliced my neck open, blood was everywhere. All my kids could say was Dad, really, on her birthday. I had bruises from the top of my shoulder covering my breast all the way down my back and torso; I had been punched in the breast the previous day while we were driving; I jumped out of the car and walked home.

I got up the next day and went to work as if nothing happened. I worked with home health, and the lady was 95, and her vision was low.

I had used liquid stitches for my neck. As I looked in the mirror and saw broken blood vessels, bruises, open wounds, I knew then I was leaving. I eventually left.

It was difficult because I didn't want a broken home. I went on for seven years trying to make it. I was ashamed to go out in public and to live in poverty. Experiencing repossessions, almost evicted.

I had to brainstorm and come up with an idea to make extra income after having two incomes for so many years. My son suffered from eczema, and I remember heating up the hard shea butter that came in small containers from the beauty store. I produced a whipped shea butter formula that eventually grew large enough to establish an online store and a storefront. The business was still stagnant, and my bills began to mount. My car was repossessed, and I was behind on my rent. I had to lease a car and move into my storefront to save money. I slept on a mattress on the floor.

I went on to move over 3,000 miles away and had a year with myself, no family, just focus. I got back on my feet. I obtained my LLC and Business License for the State of Washington and developed a CBD Line of Natural Products to add to my existing line. I had regained my confidence because my business forced me to show up. I started getting booked for speaking engagements and signing contracts across the country with wholesale agreements for my products.

My walk past hell is not over, but I am thankful for how far I have come, and I can see the light at the end of the tunnel.

About Paula Farve

Within the heart of every visionary, is a fundamental cause, to resolve, repurpose, and to reposition global needs; in order to facilitate healing, in the lives of many. Aligned with these very principles, is the compassionate professional, Paula Farve.

Paula Farve is an author, speaker, business advocate, and CEO and originator, of the **Naturally For Me Shea Butter, LLC**; a wholistic approach to multidimensional healing and skincare. Building a nationally respected brand, without any outside funding; is Paula's natural flex, and one of the many reasons she feels led to empower women and entrepreneurs with the exhortation needed, to do the same. The **SHEA QUEEN COLLECTION**; infuses essential oils, including CBD/CBG infused products; with plants grown by Paula herself, and specializes in the healing of skin rash, eczema, dryness, and other diverse ailments. Paula has created an organic empire through the power of natural products and keen entrepreneurial audacity, handling all its productivity, herself.

Paula's mantra is simple: "Naturally For Me Is Naturally For You".

Paula Farve's passion for wholistic wellness comes coupled with a great regard for higher learning, as she holds; an Associates of Occupational Science degree, a Business Administration Degree, and is both; a Nationally Certified Phlebotomist and Medical Assistant. Paula is a trusted humanitarian and has served during Operation Just Cause in Ft. Clayton Panama; in 1990 and was the first female of a group of three, to serve at the Field Artillery Ball. She has also served as a charismatic asset, to the Success Women's Conference, as an ambassador, and is inspired by the need to serve women whole heartedly.

When she is not out servicing global consumers through therealsheaqueen.com, Paula seeks to live a life that echoes hope to women, needing a new start in their lives. Paula is a celebrated member of her communal body, a beloved mother, grandparent, and friend.

Paula Farve. | Leader. | Innovator. | Advocate.
E-mail: Naturallyforme100@gmail.com
Website: www.therealsheaqueen.com

My Daddies Waited on Me to Go

by Crystal A. Hairston

For me, life has not been a crystal stairway and this chapter is not even a snippet of the Hell I have walked past, but it was a honor to have two daddies to love me truly. It was a blessing in disguise.

It wasn't until it was time for me to get my license that I learned my identity. I learned that the dad and mom I always knew as my parent Walter and Maggie Young, were not my biological parents. My name was not Crystal Young but Crystal Hairston. I had already experienced so much pain in my sixteen years of life I didn't think it could get any worse.

After learning my true identity, almost every year, I would learn something new. After a chain of events, I soon knew who my biological father was, Terry Withers. When Terry learned that my birth mom didn't abort me as she said she did, he was furious. It was a bittersweet moment. He was happy to have me but angry he had missed out on so much of my life.

Terry took me to meet my younger twin sisters, and I developed a loving relationship with all three of them. He introduced me to the bulk of his family, and I even went to a few family Thanksgiving and Christmas dinners. Terry was happy to have me in his life.

It appeared I was adapting to having two dads, but deep down inside, I felt as though I was betraying the daddy I had always known and felt as though I was bringing shame to my birth mother. When the feelings started weighing me down, I started distancing myself from Terry. I eventually shut him out of my life completely.

The daddy I always knew as a daddy was my everything. My mom, who I always thought was my mom, passed away when I was five years old. She was unable to have kids and had raised only one other child from birth. They were foster parents.

Since my older sister and I were newborns, she was able to call her own. When she passed away, Daddy vowed to her that he would keep and raise me. He always made me feel like a princess. It took a few years, in which some of them I experienced a lot of trauma, for him to raise me with minimum help daily. For the sake of my well-being, he did it. I was a true daddy's girl. I could not imagine life without him.

In October of 1998, Daddy started staying in his room the majority of the time. During this time of year, he would usually be preparing for hunting season. He started losing weight, would hardly eat, and slept a lot. I would try to get him to go to the hospital, but he would say, "No, I am alright." I knew that was not true because he was beginning not to even look like himself. I eventually was able to convince him to go to the hospital. After sitting there for a little over 3 hours, the doctor let me know that he had a mass in his stomach the size of a volleyball. He advised the mass was connected to his pancreas, gallbladder, and liver, and the chances were that it was cancer. The next morning, the doctor confirmed that it was cancer and that it was very aggressive. I was heart-broken and didn't know what to think or feel. Daddy had a proxy that indicated he didn't want any treatment or procedures to prolong his life. I felt lifeless.

Four weeks had passed, and Dad was still in the hospital. My sister Vivian and I were alternating shifts. Family members were coming in town to visit him, but at this point, he was barely speaking or opening his eyes. The only time he was guaranteed to open his eyes was when I came into the room. Saturday, December 19, 1998, my oldest sister Jean and my aunt Bea pulled me outside his room and said, "Chris, you are going to have to let him go." I asked them what they meant.

They said, "You are holding him back. You need to tell him it's okay to go."

I didn't understand it at the time as I do now, but I did what they asked me to do. I went into his room. I told him he had raised me, and I couldn't stand to see him in pain, and it was okay for him to go. He looked at me and nodded his head. Shortly afterward, our pastor came and prayed, and at the end of the prayer, Daddy said AMEN loudly.

The nurse called me the next morning around 4:30 and said the family needs to come to the hospital because his vitals were decreasing.

When I got to the hospital, Daddy looked sound asleep. All the swelling had gone down, and his skin looked so soft and smooth. I walked over to him and called his name, grabbed his hand, kissed him on the forehead, and he did not open his eyes. I stormed out of the room and went into the family waiting room. I was upset with myself for telling him it was ok to go. After calming down, I went back into his room, and as soon as I sat in the chair beside the head of his bed, he reached over as if he was trying to say something to me, but he took his last breath. The feeling I had was unexplainable.

Terry reached out to me after finding out about my daddy's passing. He let me know that he understood it was hard to adapt to my identity with all that had been unveiled. Terry explained how hard it was for him and how it has hurt him so much. I knew that Terry loved me without question or doubt, and all he wanted was for me to be a part of his life. I was so broken and could hardly keep myself together. I could still could not mentally handle it, so I shut him out of my life once again.

November 22, 2011, my cousin Margo called to tell me that the doctor had given Terry a week or less to live. It had been a little over two years since I last spoke to Terry on the phone. He told me that he had been diagnosed with cancer, but the treatments worked, and he was getting married. I instantly started having flashbacks of all the times he cried to me because he just wanted to be a part of my life. I let my feelings stand in the way. Terry was a victim of what my birth mother and maternal did and did not deserve that.

The next day, I located where he lived and went to his house. When I walked in the door, as soon as our eyes made contact, he dropped his head. I went over to him, hugged him, apologized for not being there and letting him in, and in a soft-tone, he said, "it's okay babe, you are here now."- He introduced me to his wife Karen, then he and just sat there talking and laughing. Out of the blue, Terry said, "-

Well I can die now. All I was waiting on was to see you." I said, please don't say that. God can change your situation around.

As I drove down the highway on the way home, I was full of regret. I prayed for his healing so that I can give him all the time he wanted with me. I had been home about 5 minutes when his wife called to tell me that Terry had started having trouble breathing and he was going to the hospital.

When I got to the hospital, he was still in the emergency room. I was allowed to go back to his room, where he laid with a ventilator in him. I grabbed his hand and was uncontrollably crying with a heart and mind full of regrets. I kept saying, "Terry, I am sorry, Terry, I'm sorry," he squeezed my hand lightly. I then thought I was going to lose it. Before leaving to go home, I stayed at the hospital with the family until he was in his room.

The next morning his wife Karen called and asked if I could return to the hospital because they were taking him off the ventilator. When I went into his room, I witnessed the same change in his appearance when Daddy passed. He had no swelling, and his skin looked so smooth and soft. The twins and I went over to him together. We each said our final words, then shortly after, the ventilator was removed. I don't remember the exact minutes it took his heart to stop beating, but it wasn't long.

There is death after life, and we grieve differently. Daddy and Terry's deaths struck me the same, but differently. Daddy needed my okay to go, and Terry just requested my presence.

The dad I always knew as Daddy; I miss him dearly. I will forever cherish the love he gave me as if I was his own, and the morals and values he instilled in me contribute to the woman I am today.

If I could do it all over again, I would make sure that both of my dad's felt equally loved. I would be calling Terry "daddy" and accepting the true love he desired to give me. Despite me shutting down the Hairston and Withers family for years have shown as much love as I have let them. I have allowed too much time to pass and lost more family members from my bad choices when all they want to do is love me. My birth mother can continue to deny me, but it's time I take my mask off, boldly walk into my identity, and enjoy time with my family while I still have time.

You can never get time back, so, despite life adversity, accept and love the ones that love you and don't let anything stand in the way. Love is one of the best gifts from God.

"Never ignore a person that loves, cares, and misses you because one day you may wake up and realize you lost the moon while counting the stars."

SLEEP IN PEACE, DADDIES.

About Crystal A. Hairston

Ms. Crystal A. Hairston is a woman of God, a certified life coach, speaker, and entrepreneur on the move. She has cooperated for over 30 years in customer service in call center settings, playing many roles and ending my career in cooperate office settings as one of the leaders. Crystal has always encouraged and empowered her peers and friends through life adversity. She also mentors youth and young adult women. She calls them her "Gems" She has a strong passion for helping others, getting them to their next point in life. Crystal faced a lot of life experiencing trauma and is very passionate about assisting others to believe in themself. Crystal has transitioned from the cooperate world settings to relentlessly motivate and empower people and know they can be the person they dream of and never give up.

Ms. Crystal A. Hairston is the CEO of ELLE RÊVE By Crystal A. Hairston LLC, Walterboysss LLC, author, and motivational speaker ready to be fully activated. ELLE RÊVE will soon be launching coaching and mentoring programs, fashion boutique, planning, and event business. She is also the CEO, and Founder Walterboysss LLC was created in 2017 after Crystal went back to her childhood neighborhood and re-purchased the inherited home she was raised in and lost. After purchasing the home Crystal, noticed the community was not family-oriented like she remembers. Crystal then started buying additional dwellings in the block to rehabilitate the neighborhood. The project is ongoing where even in her transition from the cooperate world, she has continued her vision with others' support. With this project's Crystal wants to open up a community center to support youth and young adults in different development areas.

Ms. Crystal A Hairston is also a part-time Director of Human Resource for Innovation Health Care Solutions. She has two daughters and three grandsons. Her oldest is a hard-working leader and the mother of three handsome sons known as the Walterboysss and the heart of Crystal. Her youngest is an aspiring doctor with a passion for dance and attends Spelman college.

ELLE RÊVE means "She Dreams" She, Crystal, dreams and turns those dreams into reality.

Business website: ellerevebycrystalahairston.com
Business e-mail: Email: info@ellerevebycrystalahairston.com

Overcoming Trauma Through Inspiring Others

by Dr. Zakiya O. Mabery

ealing trauma (s) from the past, whether mental, emotional, financial, or physical, could take months, years but for me, it's taking
a lifetime. For decades I have been focusing on leaving behind
many deep emotional scars.

Quite often, support groups, workshops, self-help books, and
years of therapy are just making micro-progressions in me. These activities cause me to pause, resonate with words on a deeper level and continue to feel a mustard seed size of self-compassion from each of these
activities. Thankful for impactful activities to aid in my recovery from
several traumatic events and healing. Can you relate?

When I was about seven years old, a family friend's son who was
almost double my age would touch me in places he shouldn't. He was
pretending to tickle me. I never told my parents about this molestation
because my parents were so close to the parents. I was afraid and concerned about my father's military career and hurting my mother. Eventually, when I was in high school, my parents reconnected with this
family. I learned the perpetrator was in prison. I felt safer. Only to be
sexually attacked a few years later by a man when I was still a teenager.
Much of that time in my life is a blur. I remember bits and pieces of the
trial. I recall struggling in school and then being placed in special education, which was a huge blow to my fragile ego, self- concept and self-
esteem. Rosa, my therapist, helped me sort through my feelings. Ms.
Cuffee was my special education teacher who believed in my success.
My parents were my advocates, and I had a small circle of trusted
friends such as Jill and Sherrice that I confided in. I was so ashamed. In
addition, I had these new 'labels' I was grappling with a learning disability,

rape victim, and misdiagnosis from the psychiatrist. I really had no clue who I was or where my life was headed.

Eventually, I obtained my bachelor's degree in psychology with the goal to obtain a Ph.D. in clinical psychology so I could help others who experienced trauma. That goal changed after functioning in the capacity of a mental health counselor and losing a client to suicide. I shifted gears and began to focus on the career field of Human Resource (HR) Management and obtained my master's degree in management and leadership. Ultimately, being awarded a Ph.D. in leadership.

Little did I know that even working in HR and equal, employee opportunity (EEO) would not shield me from encountering some very flawed, hurt, angry, and toxic individuals. I just learned from my therapist Alexis in 2020 about identifying unsafe individuals. These individuals (unsafe people) from my lived experience are in the church, in our professional organizations, in civic organizations, online attempting to coach individuals, and they are in our families, unfortunately. Yes, I have encountered trauma from each one of these items listed. Safety is defined as the state of being safe, freedom from the occurrence of risk of injury, danger, or loss.

When something traumatic happens, it changes the story of your entire world. Flashbacks come in various forms. From thoughts, feelings or very vivid dreams. I have complex PTSD due to numerous traumatic events.

I love one of my family members specifically, though I must protect my emotional health and my brand by limiting my interactions with him and his oldest daughter. I decided this after one particular unprovoked physical attack and numerous verbal attacks that went beyond just a family disagreement. I no longer feel safe around these family members. It is my hope one day that my family recognizes the extreme pain and deep wounds from these family members. **The victim is not responsible for the actions of the aggressors.** Read that last sentence *again*. It is important for my family and others to understand domestic violence can occur from a family member which is not of a sexual nature. Domestic Violence includes physical violence, emotional violence, psychological violence, spiritual violence, cultural violence, verbal violence financial abuse and verbal abuse.

Thus, I will give you three ways to protect your emotions and mental health.

First, recognize moreover understand trusting individuals after traumatic events can be very difficult. One's beliefs influence behaviors. So, pay attention to the traits of unsafe individuals. What are individuals saying? Moreover, what are their actions? I have learned that unsafe individuals tend to be quite defensive, self-righteous, extremely critical, deceitful, apologize without changing their behaviors; they attempt to flatter you vice talking to you; these individuals demand trust/respect without earning it and are stagnant instead of growing. Unsafe individuals often avoid closeness and bonding with others and usually are laser-focused on themselves. They do not have the ability to empathize with others. Any of these characteristics are huge red flags, whether it appears in a romantic relationship, platonic friendship, with a family member, coworker, supervisor, sorority sister, fraternity brother, or clergy. Pay attention and look at the character as the main factor in healthy relationships. I recommend distancing yourself from unsafe individuals.

Second, surround yourself with safe individuals. You know individuals who accept you just as you are and individuals who help you reach your goals and, ultimately, your destiny. Some individuals give you opportunities to grow and urge you to love yourself and push you to be a better version of yourself; encourage you to navigate stressful situations without sharing your issues or concerns with others. These individuals are a part of your tribe, as I call it. Embrace your tribe, thank them and assist them with life's curveballs. It's interesting how individuals want to be supported, but they do not often support others. Things that make me go "hmm," what about you?

Third, practice mindfulness. Mindfulness is the basic human ability to be fully present in the moment, aware of where you are and what you are doing. As an individual who sees the benefits in my own life from practicing mindfulness, I became a certified mindset coach to assist others.

In addition to being a certified mediator, these skills help shift thinking patterns. The techniques used are merging mediation with other activities has helped me and others have fewer panic attacks. I believe mindfulness has the potential to transform social change.

As it's more than a practice, it can be engrained into our daily lives with consistency. It sparks innovation, clear minds, reduces stress, anxiety, and negative emotions most of all, it helps me cool down. Simple techniques such as breathing exercises, stretching, and going outside to get some good ole vitamin D for a few moments are all examples of practicing mindfulness.

Experiencing trauma as a child or adult affects how individuals process information. Suppose the trauma occurred to one's child. In that case, it depends on the child's parents' (of a child, adolescent, or adult child) coping behaviors, understanding dealing with complex emotions of how they handle the situation (s). Most parents do their best with the skills they have. I encourage parents to obtain additional skills to assist their child, self, or a loved one who experienced traumatic events. It doesn't matter the parent's career or educational level; I encourage the individual to remain teachable (as my Daddy says).

It's important to note I battle suicide idolizations; I am being 100 percent vulnerable in hopes those reading this understand how deep the wounds are. For me knowing I am impacting others in a positive way gives me a little hope to keep going. When I grace my virtual stage for #Gamechangerchat and other platforms, I am encouraged by the questions, comments by participants and panelists. Stories of individuals' past trauma assist with my own healing. Please remember you never know what someone has been through or is currently going through, so don't assume, and I contend practice kindness. Depression, anxiety, post-traumatic stress disorder (PTSD), and other mental health disorders are diagnosed by a doctor; they are not adjectives. These terms should not be used to describe something, for example, "The weather is acting Bipolar this week." That statement is not appropriate. I teach my clients about other microaggressions that affect marginalized individuals and groups. I wish I had a dollar for every time I have been told, "you don't look disabled." Words matter. Words hurt.

Yes, this chapter was just the "Cliff Notes" abbreviated version of my actual walk-through hell. I invite you to continue to follow me on my journey called life as I reveal more, grow, and inspire others. Almost every day, I work on re-establishing safety, healing, and identifying triggers.

About Dr. Zakiya Mabery

Dr. Zakiya Mabery is an international motivational speaker, best-selling author and certified mindset coach. She is committed to inspiring and equipping for forward thinking individuals with the tools to courageously share their authentic voice, their diverse story, and their subject matter expertise. Dr. Mabery provides specialized inclusion training for corporate, nonprofits and government organizations, stressing the importance of intersectionality.

As a prolific writer, Dr. Mabery is the co-author and author of several publications including, "The Humans Behind The Resources." Dr. Mabery has written a book solo called, "The Complete Guide to: Diversity, Inclusion in the Age of COVID-19 First Edition," which will be available this spring. Her distinct perspectives have been shared on some of the world's most prestigious media platforms including Great Day Washington (CBS), Good Morning Washington (ABC), Black News Channel (BNC), KRON 4 News and many more.

First Annual 'The Thrive Summit' will soon be in October 2021, go to https://thethrivesummit.net for more information.

Business Email: DEI@TheZakiyaMabery.com
Website: Bglobaldiversity.com

My Bonus Kids Saved My Life!

by Brenda Young

What if doctors told you that you could never have kids? What if you found out that you have a condition with no cure or a condition that has an unknown cause? What if you are too scared to keep trying? Guess what, you can survive! I believe God built women to be survivors of anything.

Every girl dreams of having a family of her own; unfortunately for me, I cannot have children of my own (God has the final say-so on that one). In 2013 sitting in the doctor's office, my doctor walked the room to tell my husband and me that my lab work came back; it concludes that I have Polycystic Ovarian Syndrome. A condition that makes it extremely difficult for women to bear children, among other things. At that moment, all I heard was, Mrs. Young, you will not be able to have children. Everything else faded into the background. NUMB! I immediately felt extremely numb. As the tears rolled down my face, I looked at my husband, fighting back the tears being strong for me. No man wants to see his wife in shambles. The strength he has for me when I am down is impeccable.

So now what? The doctor goes on to tell us about different procedures that could work. Immediately I decided that I did not want to go through life being a guinea pig to trial and error. The devastation sent me into a deep depression about life because I was 31 years old, being told that I would never be able to have the connection in life that most women want. As the years went by, I learned to deal with what was going on with my body. Having to go through several different tests, including being tested for cancer, I did not want to go through life being poked and pulled on by doctors.

The worst part of it all was losing my career in the Navy because I couldn't maintain 140lbs at 5'1. It all started to make sense. Polycystic

Ovarian Syndrome makes it harder for women to lose weight. For years I would lose five or 10lbs then pack on 20. Lose five, then gain 15. I was working out every day, sometimes two or three times a day. I was in the gym before work, at lunch, and in boxing class after work. I was in overdrive, but nothing I was doing was working. So now I work out to maintain a healthy lifestyle.

To walk a mile in my shoes, you would have to wake up most days uncomfortable. Looking in the mirror was slim because I did not like the excess weight that I packed on that was extremely hard to get off. Not to mention the irregular menstrual cycle, going months or even years without a natural cycle. There was a point that I was on my cycle from July 31st until September 8th, 39 days (about one and a half months) straight. This was the scariest time of my life because I just knew I was headed for a blood transfusion and an emergency surgery to stop the bleeding. Thankfully, I did not have to go that route.

I couldn't leave the house. I would have to carry a suitcase with extra clothes because I was messing up all of my pants. When I went to work, I stayed in my office because I was scared of walking too far and having an accident. I was safe because the bathroom was 20 feet away.

By now, I had been to the doctor's office ten times. Within 30 days, my doctor said it was time for emergency surgery. My husband said, "No, let's get a second opinion from a different doctor."

We went to see another physician, who explained that because I had not had a cycle in three years, my body was shedding off three years of waste and to let it run its course. That wasn't what I wanted to hear because I was miserable. After being on a cycle for 39 days, I realized the emotional toll my condition had put on my body, my mind, and my spirit was depressing. It was time for a change I wanted so much more out of life than to be depressed about my health and wellness. I could no longer carry the emotional baggage.

Despite my husband constantly telling me that I was beautiful on the inside, I was crying. I wanted to feel good about myself as I did before being told that I have Polycystic Ovarian Syndrome. I spent so many years hiding behind my smile. I learned to deal with life as it came my way. Knowing the possibility of me having my own biological children were slim only made me love my bonus children more (we do not use the word "step"). When I married my husband, I married the best kids in the world who love me unconditionally. Although I would love to have a child of my own, being the best bonus mom is the most important aspect of life for me. I try my best to be the best example possible for them.

While riding in the car one day, I asked our oldest daughter how she felt about me. It is extremely important to me that we know how our children feel. I honestly believe if we allowed her to use profanity, she would have cursed me out. She said, "WHAT YOU MEAN? YOU MY MOMMA! You feed me; you buy me clothes, take me to the doctor and love me. What more could I ask for?"

For hours we just talked about our relationship, and she made my heart smile. It is important for me to have conversations with my kids. I had a conversation with our oldest son and asked him why he always makes sure I'm okay when I don't feel good. He gave me the same answer as my daughter. He simply said, "YOU MY MOMMA AND I LOVE YOU. I don't like it when you don't feel good."

These are the moments that make me realize that I am extremely blessed. I may not be able to physically have children; however, God blessed me with four amazing kids. No matter what goes on in life, they know that they can call me, I am coming. These children saved my life.

They saved me from beating myself up about something that may not have been meant for me and may not have been a part of my purpose in this life. My blessing of having children came in a different form, and I realize that it is all right for me to give them 100% of my love all the time. I pray for them when they are in my care, and I pray for them even harder when they are not. I am their mother too.

My husband and I discussed with our older children the idea of adoption. While most parents try to make the best decision for the family, it was vital for me to understand how my kids felt about me wanting to adopt. They are fully on board with the idea of adopting another child and often joke about how this new kid can't be older than them.

Although this option is still on the table, I am embracing our children's love and affection.

It is essential to know that it is okay to feel however you want to about the changes. I've never wanted to be depressed about my medical circumstances, and it happened. Having a support system and prayer helps ease the pain. In the back of my heart and mind, I wish I could bear children; I realized that my health and well-being are so important. My husband put it to me best. He said, "Baby, it would do us no good for us to have another child, and I lose my wife in the process." I am so grateful for those words because he spoke nothing but the truth to me. He was right. I did not want to fight for my life trying to have a child.

I am blessed, and I owe it to my husband and four children for helping me see that I am going to be okay. I am loved by the five of them with every ounce of joy that they can give me. My heart is so full. I am a survivor who is blessed to be able to tell what I've been through. I am not one to question God's will and plan for my life. I pray often and thank God every day for being able to stand through the hardest time of my life. I might have had to walk through hell, but I didn't have to do it alone.

About Brenda Young

The gift of inspiration is one of the most significant traits of a natural born leader. Having the courage to live out values of integrity, discipline, and transparency, in the face of a generation, on the verge of malfeasance; is an honored rarity, assumed by few. Leading by example, is the compassionate professional, Brenda Young.

Brenda Young is an author, women's advocate, business generalist, CPR Instructor and CEO and Founder of **Babs Jewels LLC**, a multidimensional retail and women's support specialty, focused on providing various buyers, with a diverse selection, in jewelry-based products and other inspirational resources.

Brenda's Mantra is simple: She believes her sole purpose in life is to inspire and be inspired by women, uplifting one another.

Brenda Young is no stranger to inspirational leadership, as she has served many years in the armed forces, bringing high honors to the field of servant leadership, through her acts of service in both, Naval expedition and Corrections Facility Leadership. In addition to servant leadership, Brenda has shown a regard for higher learning, having earned her associate degree in Applied Business Office Technology, from Antonelli College, in 2015; accompanied by achieving honors of perfect attendance and making the Deans List of academic excellence.

Brenda has also been recognized her many contributions in servant leadership, having earned the National Defense Service Medal, Global War on Terrorism (Service and Expeditionary) Medal, two Navy Sea Service Deployments, two Navy Good Conduct Medals, a Navy Rifle Qualification Ribbon and Medal in 2009: A Navy Pistol Qualification Ribbon and Medal Sharpshooter, Navy and Marine Corps Achievement Medal, Navy E Ribbon, and a US Navy Honorable Discharge.

When Brenda Young is not out, changing the world through the gift inspiration, she is trusted member of her local community and a loving member of her family.

Brenda Young. | Leader. | Advocate. | Inspiration list.
Business email- mrsbrendayoung@babsjewels.com
Business page- www.facebook.com/babsvisions

God's Amazing Grace

by Valerie McKnight-Brooks

"Our Father, who art in Heaven. Hallowed be thy name.
Thy kingdom come, thy will be done, on Earth as it is in Heaven.
Give us this day our daily bread."
Matthew 6: 9-11

*I*t is amazing how far back I can remember some of what seems like the smallest details that helped shape my life. The Lord's Prayer and the song Amazing Grace stand out the most. One day, I was five or six years old; I was standing on the back porch on a hot summer day. As I gazed into the sunlight and noticed my Grandpa bent over working in his garden, humming Amazing Grace how sweet the sound. My Grandpa was my rock as a child. He was one of my greatest inspirations.

"Valerie, Valerie," he called, and I ran off the porch.

"I am right here, Grandpa."

He said, "I have something for you, my sweet grand," and passed me a large pail of strawberries. I thanked him, and he asked me to come inside so we could wash them.

As early as five or six years old, I can remember singing songs in church before my Grandpa's sermons. He was a pastor and a military veteran. The church members complimented me after singing. I recall some of them saying that I was a great singer and would one day be a preacher. Little did they I know; they saw something in me I did not see in myself.

My mother was a woman of small stature, smart, and stern. Mother was a hard worker. She worked as a housekeeper and believed in keeping things neat and in order, and I was raised that way. My mother taught me early in life to never look for handouts and get things myself.

My father was only a picture on a wall. I never got a chance to meet or know him. They divorced when I was three months old. Mom never talked much about him but did say I looked and acted like him quite often, and to be honest, I really did not want to hear that from her or anyone else. Not knowing him left a void.

I was teased as a child because I was dark-skinned and began to feel ugly. I was also a sickly child. I had to deal with Bronchitis, asthma and was often hospitalized. As I look back, I know my Grandpa understood me not having my father in my life so lovingly filled the void. He would read scriptures to me, prayed with and for me, and songs that I still apply to my life today.

My Grandpa would take me with him to do his trading and VA appointments. One day he told me I could not go with him to see the doctor, and I was hurt, but I reluctantly agreed and fought back the tears. When he pulled into the driveway to let me out of the car, he slumped over the steering wheel. I called out to him and shook him, but he did not respond. I called my Grandma, and it was too late; he was gone. I was devastated, lost, alone, more angry, and immeasurable pain.

At this point, I am feeling angry with God, everyone, and myself. At this time, I prayed very little. I did not think the Lord heard my prayers anyway, nor was I on his priority list. But oh, was I wrong.

"The Lord is my Shepherd; I shall not want…"
Psalm 23:1

As I entered adolescence, my soul became numb and hardened even more because of what I had endured to this point. I became clinically depressed. I cried all the time; anxiety caused me to yell and scream until I fell asleep. My mother eventually got me to counseling. I was prescribed medication that made me feel catatonic, but I was convinced that she was trying to have me hauled off to some facility. I tried to commit suicide twice and started drinking heavily to numb the pain. I was diagnosed with clinical depression; I was in a dark place.

When I was sixteen years old, I met someone who stole my heart. He was older than me and smart. He said all the things I needed to hear. I fell for him. I enjoyed being around him. Not long after we were together, he began to abuse me by slapping, choking, kicking, and dragging me across the floor but said that he loved me each time he did it, or he was having a bad day, or I caused it to happen. He said he would not do it again, and I stayed because I believed he loved me. My mother told me that I was not ready for a serious relationship, but I did not listen.

After I finished high school and got pregnant, the abuse continued. I remember during an argument, and he drove to a bridge. He drags me out of the car, choking me. He held my head over the bridge and told me he would throw me off, and I would never be found if I tried to leave him or be with another man. I was scared to death of him.

Right before I gave birth to my son, my abuser went to jail. My son weighed 2lbs and 5 oz. He was given a 40% chance to live. I cried out to God to save my son because now I had someone to live for. When I saw him in the incubator clinging to life, I had to get out of this dark place that life had trapped me in. I had to be a good stable mother for my son, my glimmer of hope in the darkness.

> **"No temptation has overtaken you except what is common to mankind. And God is faithful; he will not let you be tempted beyond what you can bear. But when you are tempted, he will also provide a way out so that you can endure it."**

Corinthians 10:13

My son's father got out of jail and came to see his son, and we got into an argument. I asked him to leave. He started beating and choking me again, but this time, I fought back. I looked into his eyes while fighting him and saw some unrecognizable. I only saw evil. I started praying the Lord's prayer while being choked. I could not breathe but heard gurgling sounds, and everything got quiet. I woke up to a voice calling me, "Valerie, Valerie." I looked up and saw my Grandpa standing over me. I was crying so hard. I reached for his hand, and he said, "GET UP!" He used to say that to me all the time when I fell off a bike. I was trying to talk to and reach for him but to no avail. When I stood up, he was gone.

I limped to my son's room to check on him, and he was asleep; I thanked God. I went to the restroom and looked in the mirror. My face was a mess. One of my eyes was swollen shut and black, a dark red spot was in one of my eyes, my sides were hurting me. Every breath was painful. My nails were broken to the skin, my top lip was swollen and was cut. I remember thinking at that moment, no amount of makeup can cover this up.

"For everything, there is a season."

Ecclesiastes 3

I prayed, and suddenly, the peace and love of God came over me. I realized I was blessed. For the first time, I could think clearly. I felt peace within, and my love for my son inspired me. I was on my way and growing gracefully.

"Forgive and Live…"

"And forgive us our trespasses, and those that trespass against us and lead us not into temptation but deliver us from evil."

Matthew 6: 12-14

I repented and asked God to forgive me my trespasses against others and help me forgive all those that trespassed against me. My healing started.

"I praise you for I am fearfully and wonderfully made, marvelous are thy works and that my soul knoweth quite well."

Psalm 139: 14

Today I embrace my identity and understand my purpose. I am free indeed. God is my father and has been with me all along. I am confident and at peace in my ebony skin. I am uniquely designed by God. I am blessed and beautiful. I am a daughter of the king. Today, I understand why Grandpa always hummed God's amazing grace.

About Valerie McKnight-Brooks

Attaining an outstanding quality of life is not surrendered to materialistic gain but rather an introspective relationship with God, people, and self. Personifying this awareness is the compassionate, professional, Valerie McKnight-Brooks.

Valerie McKnight-Brooks is an author, advocate, licensed health care professional with 25 years' experience, singer, song writer, and multidimensional entrepreneur, with a passion for the advancement of people. Valerie understands the importance of living a life driven by a mandate to serve others. As the granddaughter of an ordained minister, Valerie was raised with a deep connection with God and often attests that it was through the strength of that foundation that she was able to endure many dark days. Her early days were spent burdened by bouts of clinical depression, anxiety, attempts of suicide, and domestic violence, all by which Valerie views as opportunities when her faith was brought to the forefront of her life, in order to preserve lives today.

Valerie's mantra is clear! She is inspired by seeing others forgive, heal, and win!

The challenges of her past problems are no match against Valerie's will to achieve great things.

In 1995, she obtained her nursing degree from Hinds Nursing Allied in Jackson, MS. In 1998, she was ordained as an evangelist under Bishop Clarence Gray. Valerie also showed a great respect for higher learning and obtained her associate degree in theology at Christian Life School of Theology in Marietta, GA in 2004.

Valerie is a gifted singer/songwriter with an electrifying voice. She released her first professional recording in 2009 and signed with Ecko Records in 2015. Through the years Valerie has released 4 albums and one single that is heard on the radio throughout the US and abroad. She is employed with Prime Care Nursing and in 2020, she was honored and awarded for her excellence in service.

Valerie is no stranger to her local community and has served in previous years, women's homeless shelter, prison ministries, homeless shelters, and communal programs for depression/mental illness. Valerie has also used her philanthropic and creative passions in her faith-based community, serving often in intercessory prayer, music ministry, evangelism, and outreach ministry.

When she is not advocating love and servant leadership to all the world, she enjoys biking, reading, and writing songs. She has one son, Eric Jr., two grandsons: one grandson living, Daquan and recently lost her second grandson, Eric III to an apartment fire, a loving mother Bertha Carter, three siblings, Marcus, Loretta, and David, and a cherished wife to her husband, Kenneth Brooks.

Valerie McKnight-Brooks. | Servant. | Leader. | Advocate
E-mail: vivaciousms72@gmail.com
Facebook: Valerie McKnight-Brooks

The Beauty and The Beast

by Raye Campbell

As I open my eyes, I almost pee on myself because the black thing shoved in my face looks like a gun. But it can't be a gun because he loves me, right? Rewind! Let us talk about how we got here. I consider myself a beautiful, educated, talented woman. Yet, I was allowing someone who said they loved me to hit me, to call me names, to make me feel like I was nothing. How can the man who took vows to honor and to cherish me and to protect me, all the days of my life, hurt me? Well, I will tell you. He was angry. He was angry all the time, but not with me. He was angry with himself. Why? He had a failed career as he had managed to get kicked out of the military. He was a product of the foster care system and he was mad at me because I grew up with both of my parents. I thought that my smile, my charm, and my beauty would be able to tame the beast that I called my husband.

My life was a living hell. But, on the outside looking in, others wanted to be like me. But why? They just did not know that I spent many days looking for the perfect concealer to cover up black eyes and bruises. They did not know that my bank account was empty just hours after I got paid because my husband felt like I did not deserve the money that I earned. They did not know that the nice car that I drove was on the verge of being repossessed. How would they know? I put on a happy face and smiled through the pain that kept me up at night.

I was in the United States Air Force. I loved what I did, and I was good at it, too. I dealt with a lot on the job. Shift work, long hours, loud planes. Yet, I would rather be at work preparing to fight foreign terrorists instead of the domestic terrorist that shared the same bed and last name as me.

How could he be so mean to someone who was so sweet to him? I cooked, I cleaned, I gave him sex when he wanted it. Hell, I even went to work when he did not. Well, I had to figure it out and figure it out fast. I had to figure out a way to make the hitting stop. I had to make him love me again because this was not the man I fell in love with. I got it! What better way to soften him up than to have a baby, right? Wrong! At first, he was happy. He was nice and sweet. The yelling and name-calling stopped. I did it! He was running my bathwater, rubbing my feet, and even asking how my day went. Little did I know he was covering up what was really going on behind the scenes.

The beast is back! We were sitting and eating some french fries and when I had finished all of mine, I reached over to his plate to get just one more for me and the little person growing inside of me. I felt the sharpest pain. But it was not a contraction - it was coming from my hand. Why does my finger feel broken? He had bent my fingers back so hard and slapped me for getting one of his fries without asking. I was in shock. Why was he so mad about a french fry? Before I knew it, the scene turned into something like out of a horror movie. I was levitating! Yes, he had grabbed me by my neck, pinned me up against the wall, and for what? It was not about the last of his French fries. It was about his secrets. The secrets that were about to come to light. He was living a double life.

He would take 30 minutes to take out the garbage. He was always changing the password on his phone and then would hide it in his clothes in his closet. But again, I am beautiful and smart! I knew something was not right. So, I went looking. And I found it. He had a girlfriend. Yes, my husband had a girlfriend. She lived out of town, but he would talk to her when I was at work. I sent all the texts and the emails to myself so that I could print them out and have proof before he tried to delete them and call me crazy. Good idea, right?

Well, now we are back to me waking up with the gun being pointed in my face. Before bed, I confronted him with what I knew. I had proof. I said, "I want a divorce." I told him to pack his things and get out. I was 8 months pregnant. I did not care. I said, "You can shoot me. I will no longer put up with this. The hurt, the lies, the abuse will be over!" His angry face changed. He did not look like the angry beast that I was used to seeing. He put the gun down and away. He started packing all of his belongings. When he was done, he handed me all the overdue bills that he was responsible for paying, but had not, along with the house key and he left.

The nightmare was over! Or was it? It really was. I no longer had to put up with the abuse from someone that was supposed to love me. Love does not hurt. I filed for divorce at 8 months pregnant. I was now a single parent. I had to figure out how I would survive and take care of my children. But with God on my side, I knew anything was possible.

I started a whole new life. I didn't look back or dwell on what I had been through. The first stop was self-love. It is so hard to love other people or know what love from others is supposed to look like If you do not start with loving yourself. I started going to the mall and buying myself nice things. I would go and get massages, take myself to lunch, and just spend time with myself. Getting to know *me* and the things that I wanted out of life started me on my self-love journey. It has been one of the best trips I have ever taken. On the journey, I learned what I will and will not accept from others. I have learned to accept my flaws and to love them. I have learned to love and accept all parts of me, even the parts that do not reflect what I want them to in the mirror. I am able to understand myself and where I fit in the world. Acceptance from myself was the starting point of self-love. The journey is ongoing, and I have committed to myself to never feel like I felt when I was married to a beast. Having the courage to face an issue is the first step towards getting help out of a terrible situation. Moving on and not dwelling on the past will set anyone on a road to healing. The past has shaped me into the person that I am today. However, I take those experiences to help me shape my and my children's present and future.

I may have touched the flaming hot fire, but I walked right past Hell.

About Raye Campbell

Born in Raleigh, NC but raised in Atlanta Ga, RayShauna Campbell who affectionally goes by the name Raye has a passion and drive for motivating and helping people. At an early stage in her life, she knew that people were her passion, as she was very involved on her college (Morris Brown College) campus. Upon graduating, Raye enlisted into the United States Air Force, traveled the world, met people from multiple facets of life. In her final assignment in the military, as an instructor, is where she knew that she had the voice and natural gift to help others.

After an untimely lightning accident in 2017, Raye had to medically retire from the Air Force and figure out her next career move. In 2019 Raye Speaks L.L.C was formed to help, motivate, and transform people all over the world. Her goal as a life coach and motivational speaker is to inspire others with her life story, to be their best and discover themselves in a way they never have. She uses her podcast to bring motivation to her clients as well as advocate for the awareness of domestic violence, suicide prevention, and veterans' homelessness. Raye is a member of Kappa Epsilon Psi Military Sorority Inc., whose mission is "Women of Service, Being of Service", and she does just that giving back to her community with Habitat for Humanity, The Salvation Army, and The Armed Forces Retirement Home. Raye is also a loving wife and mother of five.

Business e-mail: Hearrayespeak@gmail.com
Facebook: Raye Speaks.

The Re-Birth

by Shannon Hancock

In the fall of 2007, I took a short-term position in Nashville, Tennessee. I rented a room since it was going to be a temporary job assignment. The place was perfect since we all worked opposite shifts. One afternoon, as I was leaving for work, one of my roommates came in the front door looking incredibly sad and confused. I asked him, "Are you okay?" He replied, "NO" and then lunged at me yelling and screaming. He grabbed me by the neck and started punching me in the head and face. I managed to start to pull away from him a little and he grabbed me by the throat, choking me and beating me, while continuing to yell at me.

While this was going on, I knew I had to survive. I didn't want to become another statistic. I could not give up. I had my beautiful sons to live for. So, I started punching back. I was resilient as I desperately tried to peel his hands off my throat. When I pushed him back, he lunged forward and started beating me all over again. I knew I did not want to die. As he was punching me in my face, head, and arms, I started punching him and screaming for help.

As I tried to wiggle out of his grip, I ran from the doorway into the living room to the back sliding door. As I tried to figure out how to unlock the door, he grabbed the wooden curtain rod and started beating me with it - eventually breaking it over my body. As I got away and ran upstairs to try to call 911, he followed behind me and ended up breaking down the locked door to the bedroom I was hiding in and continued to punch me in the face. I fell on the floor and he started kicking and stomping on my body.

As quickly as he snapped when this started, he just stopped. He looked at me super puzzled and said, "What happened to you? You look like you need to go to the hospital." I was confused and thinking to myself, what in the hell did this man just do to me? I was so scared and just kept thinking in my head, what in the world is wrong with him? Since I had not seen this type of behavior out of him before, I was really confused. Yes, he was a roommate, but judging from his character up to this point, I knew something was seriously wrong with this man.

I called a friend and went to the hospital where I was examined and deemed okay. However, I was very broken inside and out. I kept wondering what I did that provoked this? Was there more to the story of why he would do this to me? While I was in the hospital, he rummaged through my belongings and found my banking information. He started transferring money out of my account into his account. This left me broke, homeless, and devastated. I was hungry, tired, and had nowhere to go.

After being discharged from the hospital, I was so dazed and confused about the past few days of my life. I found myself very scared and reluctant to trust anyone. I went back and forth on the idea of having to go back to that house to gather my belongings. I knew if I went back, I could face being attacked again and if I went back, I didn't want to be seen. I knew that I had one last trip to grab and carry what would fit in my car.

After a few days, I chose to sneak back and grab what I could. I started living out of my car for the next few months. Still, this left me with no money to move into a place or even a warm spot to lay my head. At this point, I was hungry, homeless, and I felt I was out of options. I was alone in a city that I had only been to a few times and I did not have many friends, family, or support systems other than the few people I had met along my journey. It was wintertime so it was cold outside. After working the second shift, I would find a place to park and rest, warming up my car as needed to keep me from freezing. The nights were long and cold. I would have to stay on the move to avoid being caught by different building securities around the city. It was hard. Many nights I would pray to God to just give me the strength to make it through or to just let me die in my sleep. I was in a very dark place in my life.

My breakthrough came one evening when I was at work. I got a call from a customer named Keith Simpson. He was asking several questions about the products and services my company offered. I explained everything to him and in the middle of the conversation he asked, "What is wrong with you?" You seem sad." I explained to him that I was fine and that I would have all the information he needed shortly. He said to call him when I got off because he needed to know what is wrong with me! Due to company policy, I knew I could not call. However, I called anyways. I left work that night and went to my little hiding spot to call him. Within a few minutes of being on the phone, I broke down. I cried and explained I was attacked by my roommate and it changed my current living situation drastically. I explained to him the beating I endured which left me in the situation I was currently in that left me homeless and hungry. I told him my financial situation as well. We talked for about an hour and he asked me to call him back the next morning.

I called this stranger the next morning and he explained to me that he was a victim of Katrina and he lost everything in the hurricane. But he was safe, and he was taking refuge in a church in New Orleans. He said he felt that he needed to help me. His kindness and wisdom pulled me out of the dark spot I was in. He paid for me to live in a hotel for a month, he provided me money to get food to eat, and he rebuilt my strength. He became not just the man on the other end of the phone, but a true friend. He believed in me and pushed me to believe in myself again. He was a true angel in disguise.

I eventually got my account to straighten out and was able to move out of the hotel. The attack put me in a dark place as I could not trust anyone. However, with the strength of God and prayer, and my will to move on, I have since recovered from my attack and rebuilt my life. I relied on prayer and my faith to nurture me to move on with my life. I walked away knowing that I made it through what I felt, at the time, was the worst thing that had ever happened to me. Even though we feel like we are living in hell, I was able to walk past it because there are still good people in the world. I encourage anyone that has been through this or something similar to keep the faith and know there is something bigger and brighter out there for you. With the strength of God, you will make it through.

About Shannon Hancock

There is nothing more powerful than the bold clarity of the human voice. Living in a society masked often as a war zone, it takes advocates, born with the courage to use their voices; in order to see meaningful progression, on our journey toward a better world. Leading by effortless example, is the energized professional, Shannon Hancock.

Shannon Hancock is an author, motivational speaker, organizational guru, and CEO and Founder of Shannon Hancock, LLC; a specialty centered around the formation of finding practical solutions, through the simplistic principles of cleaning, assortment, and organization; in order to foster space for positive thinking and personal clarity in the lives of her clients. Shannon's effervescent nature has reputed her as one of the best in the professional arena, as she is often called upon to aid in diverse leadership roles, including having been a customs broker for V Alexander & Co., and as a production manager for The Kim Jacobs Show.

Shannon's mantra is simple: **she believes in the good of all people; especially women. She anthems that with a strong soul and support from all sisters, we can take over the world; one person at a time.**

Shannon has a premier vernacular concerning women's issues, and often relies on the strength of her experience as a single mother and divorcee; as rudders helping to steer other women on their journey toward healing and the inner solace needed, to find their personal and professional voices.

When Shannon is not out advocating for the causes of women, she is a beloved member of her local professional community, and the proud mother of two sons, Tyler and Tanner.

Shannon Hancock. | Leader. | Speaker. | Women's Enthusiast.
Business website: www.shannonhancock.com
E-mail: shannon694@gmail.com

This Doesn't Happen to People Like Me

by Natalie Jones Bonner

I was the bougie baby boomer even at age 17. That has been my persona growing up. Some would say this was an over-inflated impression of myself. But me feeling this way did not keep me from getting my ass whipped.

What happened? My girls and I had just finished with Dixie Darling's practice and grabbing a bite to eat. As I approach my dorm, I see his car parked in front, lights on, engine running. I pick up my pace.

"Hey babe, sorry I am late. How's it going?" He opens the door, and I step into the open space, the door handle resting against my butt cheek. I am rambling nervously and begin to step out of the door gap. He attempts to slam the car door shut and catches my leg dead center on my shin. First, I experience the pain; then, I experience the realization that it was intentional. All he says is, "you must think I am fucking stupid."

I am dumbfounded. Did he intentionally slam that car door on my leg? No way.

You see, I experienced my first orgasm with this man. We make each other laugh, we cook together, and we lay in bed on Sundays together. We complement each other; he loves me, he wouldn't intentionally harm me, would he? I will call him when I get upstairs to make sure he is ok.

He broke up with me! But I keep calling because the thought of him being with someone else or doing "that" with someone else is too much. No one ever breaks up with me. I am the hot girl on campus. I am Miss It! Well, in my mind.

We are a couple again; normalcy has returned after the car incident. My college girl life resumes, and we never talked about that night. Because I know he could not have meant to hurt me.

The next time was brutal, vicious and it caught me totally off guard. I thought I would lose my eye from the punches to my face. The pain, coupled with the fear of more punches to follow, sent me into prayer. Dear God, what is happening? How can this be? What are the people driving beside and behind us thinking as they see him punching me relentlessly with one hand, while with precision, the other hand steadily steers the vehicle? I am curled up against the passenger side door, experiencing every punch, shielding myself as best as I can.

My crime is I did not pay the car note on my lunch break at the pay-as-you-go car lot. I went the next morning, and they would not accept the payment. They were going to repossess his precious vehicle. It was not my fault he was already 90 days behind, which triggered the repossession. My face and body received the rage of his 90-day delinquency. That night I lay alone in the apartment frightened, beaten, swollen, and bruised. I was ashamed and did not feel I could tell anyone or ask for help.

It happened again. Not only was there physical abuse, but there was also *her*. She, the one who left me a calling card of her panties and bra in my bed, wanting me to know she had sex with my husband in my bed. I should have divorced him; I didn't because I did not want to be labeled as a woman who couldn't keep her man. Think about that. I'd rather get my ass beaten in a sad marriage than have people outside my marriage think I couldn't keep him.

In retrospect, I realize that I come from a family of males who cheated on their wives, but they always took good care of their homes. That was the case for my granddad, my dad, and some of my uncles. My husband fit that mold. We always lived in nice places and had fancy stuff. Things always looked good on the outside.

I am sitting here on the couch six months pregnant, barefoot; he suspects I am planning a getaway. As he is leaving for work, my bare feet in his path, he attempts to stomp on my toes with his steel-toed boots. I move quickly, dodging his intent. That day I called friends, and they rescued me.

The family grapevine is buzzing, and he is calling everyone looking for me. My beloved grandfather does not fully understand my suffering, and he tells him where I am. He comes with his empty promises. I know he is lying, yet I return with him. Shortly thereafter, I gave birth to a son who only lived for three days.

I must escape to be safe and possibly even to be happy. I escape by joining the Navy. For my boot camp graduation, however, he visits, and we spend the night together. Now I am pregnant again.

Eventually, I end my military career, and we are living in San Diego. I know you are thinking, "how stupid can she be?" The physical abuse has ended, but the emotional abuse has been perfected. Now the affairs with other women are not hidden.

One evening I was crying quietly as I drew my son's bathwater. At the time, my son was about two. He put his little hand on my cheek and asked, "Mommy got a boo-boo?"

I did have a boo from this loveless marriage. I wouldn't stand up for myself, but I could not allow my son and my daughter to figure out that I was being abused by their father, who they adored. I'd created an elaborate façade; you see, on Fridays, he would leave and not come back until Monday sometimes. Protecting him, I stayed busy making excuses to the kids about where their dad was.

I don't know why I felt I needed to cover for him. Even today as a grown-ass woman, I retain those feelings of needing to represent a positive standard for my kids. I have never told them this about their father.

Those Navy years and the friendships built helped me to gain some bravado. I found a circle of trust. I built a tribe, a powerful support system, and I began to ask for help.

The most difficult lesson about my path to freedom was when I realized how I was complicit in how I was abused. I was silent. I was ashamed. I did not feel free to ask for help, to share my story. While the motivation to move on is because I didn't want my son or daughter to think the way their father treated me was how a woman should be treated is honest, the real reason I was able to break free is that I knew at some point I would be brave enough to help someone else by telling my story.

My Walk Past Hell, the expediency of my steps, was for us, but it really is my story. I rose above the flames of Hell to become a woman who found herself, and it is only because of that I can forgive. Yes, I forgave him. You see, it is easy to forgive when you are living in joy, the recipient of unconditional love from a man with whom I have spent the last 32 years beyond, My Walk Past Hell.

About Natalie Jones Bonner

Organic business leaders understand innovation as a quintessential component in achieving optimal opportunity. Multidimensional professional, Natalie Jones Bonner is the epitome of this defining statement.

Natalie Jones Bonner is an author, advocate, business innovator, and Co-Founder of Blue Lotus Creations, a retailer of carefully curated hemp-derived wellness products, and Champagne, Art, and CBD on Howard, a marrying of wellness and inspiration. Blue Lotus Creations has developed a fast acting, long-lasting pain management solution in its flagship product Na'Vera. Na'Vera, is a pain salve which allows clients to more effectively manage their pain, forgoing the aid of pharmaceuticals.

Natalie's mantra is two-fold; be intentional; be instrumental in spearheading Social Justice Reform, and Social Equity by challenging lawmakers to create cannabis legislation that includes minorities who have been most disenfranchised by the failed War

on Drugs. As reciprocity, these individuals must be given the opportunity at both freedom, and wealth acquisition in the cannabis industry.

Displaying an unequivocal ability to deliver on all thresholds, Natalie is no stranger in the use of professional advocacy, and its ability to facilitate lucrative benefits, for both clients and collaborators. Her tenacity to create, educate, and deliver top-tier results; is presently shown in her current role, as the SVP of Contracts at Visual Awareness Technologies, and Consulting Inc., headquarters in Tampa, FL; where Natalie's business acumen has led to the negotiation of well over 100 million dollars in Government, and Commercial contract awards.

Natalie Jones Bonner holds a Master of Art; in Procurement and Acquisition Management and is a Certified Government Contracts Manager. She is the Mississippi State Chapter President of Minorities for Medical Marijuana, and a USDA Licensed Hemp Producer. She is also a member of the Ms. Medical Marijuana Association, Ms. Industrial Hemp Association, Ms. Cannabis Trade Association, Hemp Industry Association, Ms. Gulf Coast Chamber of Commerce, Hemp Industries Association, United States Hemp Building Association, Success Women's Network, Lighthouse Business & Professional Women, Likeminded Ladies of the Gulf Coast, PowerHer, and the NAACP. Natalie has been featured in numerous trade magazine articles and news stories.

Showing no signs of stopping, Natalie remains committed to the health and wellness industry. Blue Lotus Creations' products aspire to be the "champagne" of wellness products. Natalie will continue in her quest to educate and help individuals achieve wellness through implementing the efficacies of plant medicine into their routines.

When Natalie is not out advocating for holistic approaches to wellness, and supporting Social Justice Reform and Social Equity initiatives, she is a deliberate asset to her communal body, and a cherished member of her family and friendship circles.

Natalie Jones Bonner. | Leader. | Innovator. | Advocate.
Contact: (833) 675-2818
Website: https://www.shopbluelotus.net/

"Reclaiming My Voice!"

by Dr. Josephine Harris

As a teen mother, I thought my life was like a never-ending fairy tale; boy, I was naïve. So, there I was anxious, exhaling a sigh of eagerness and relief. YES, I graduated as a single teen mother, a 19-year-old with two girls and six months pregnant with a baby boy. I was happy but not pleased after all; I was a single teen mom. After graduating from high school, I applied to a well-known law school and received an acceptance letter; I planned to go after having my baby boy. All that changed when I met Big T; I thought he was the man of my dreams. He had a look that caught my attention. He was tall, handsome with blue, green shiny eyes and a smooth walk that took your breath away. Big T was also willing to love me and be a part of my life (children). He also was lovely, gentle, and loving. Although I was loved by my family and admired by others, I thought I needed a man more to fill the void; I felt I needed him and wanted him to validate my self-worth. He would always tell me that he loved me and would be with me forever, not knowing that it might be my last time seeing and visiting my family and friends.

The fairy tale turned into my nightmare. Nine months after my son was born, we moved in together. After about six months in our two-bedroom apartment duplex, I began to feel depressed and isolated because, at this time, we only had one car, which he drove most of the time. I would have to schedule my and my children's appointments according to his schedule. If my plan did not fit his schedule, he would make me reschedule or miss appointments. He would make comments like, "You are stupid; you can't schedule the appointments correctly."

All I would do is cry and apologize for scheduling the appointments at the wrong time. It went on like this for months, unable to use the car or visit family regularly. He would want me to be with him every second and minute. I was afraid to tell my family and friends what was going. I knew that something was wrong, but I did not want to believe that I was going through this emotional and mental abuse. But I always kept a smile.

This side of me wants to be loved and desired by a man; however, my father loved me (i.e., that was a different kind of love, father-daughter love). My father was there (e.g., weekend trips and holidays), but he was not entirely in my life as a daughter needed. Because he had other children and a wife/girlfriend, he wasn't there like I wanted or needed his support.

Well, let me get back to why this nightmare began! Big T and I would hang out with his friends, who drank a lot when they were all together. But their drinking did not bother me. It was that Big T would get drunk and begin the name-calling, "BITCH," "STUPID ASS," and "SLUT." The disbelief and look on his friends' faces would be of shock. They didn't believe that he would speak to me so disrespectfully. I would utter to his friends, "I am Ok," knowing that I was hurting deep down inside. His name-calling continued throughout the night, even going to the car. Keep in mind; he was too drunk to drive home, so I had to drive home!

Now, you ask, "Why didn't you leave?" That's easier said than done. I wanted to leave, but I had no car, no money, and was ashamed to go back home because I was considered the family's smart girl who wanted to be a lawyer. And I rejected the acceptance letter from law school.

Well, let me finish the story. It gets worse before it gets better! Late that night, we picked up the kids from my mother's house. My mother asked, "Is everything ok, Jo?"

I responded, "Yes, "I'm fine," and we went home.

He did not say one word when the kids were in the car, but he started to cuss at me and then at the kids when we got home. I believe my oldest daughter was about five years old. I told my daughter to take her younger sister and brother into the room and not come out no matter what you hear.

This is where it all ended. He started calling me a bitch and saying that I was a bad example of a mother. He also started pushing me and yelling at me. Then we went from the living room to the bedroom and onto the stairs. For the first time in my face, he struck me so hard that I fell down the stairs. I did not know that he had a small knife, and I realized that I had a small cut on my face. He started weaving the knife in the air like he was going to cut me. Somehow, I had enough time to go to the closet to get his handgun. He was unaware that I knew it was there; it was loaded. The kids were upstairs in their room with the door locked. He charged at me with the knife, and I shot at him, missing his right ear by inches. However, the neighbor called the law enforcement with all the chaos going and the shots they heard in our house.

The kids were crying, screaming, and yelling, "Mommy, Mommy, Mommy, are you ok?"

That was when I knew that it was time for me to "Reclaim my Voice!" I was silent, ashamed, useless, and dishonored for a long time. So, when the law enforcement arrived, I began to speak up for the first time and tell them what happened and had been happening in my house. This was not the first time that law enforcement had come to our residence, but I said to myself, "this is it ...my truth...Reclaim my Voice!"

I am not perfect, but who is? You don't have to be ashamed or embarrassed! You don't have to be silent! You have a voice; claim it! So, to anyone who feels silent, humiliated, mortified, or belittled, it is time for you to speak up, speak out, and reclaim your voice!

About Dr. Josephine Harris

Modern day superheroes are not the ones we familiarize in motion pictures, but rather the quintessential professionals; gifted with a sharp sense of servant leadership, willing to show up greatly; in the lives of those who need it most. Yielded to this profound ethic; is the multifaceted advocate, Dr. Josephine Harris.

Dr. Josephine Harris is an author, philanthropist, behavior analyst, serial entrepreneur, and CEO/Founder of Calming Minds LLC, a multidimensional coaching practice, helping clients to connect with the mind, body, and soul, by way of inspiration, facilitation, coaching, and other dynamic mechanisms. Bringing a vast portfolio of uncompromising skillsets and certifications to her practice, within the realms of: Addiction counseling, Intervention programing, Domestic Violence, individual and group psychotherapy, and many more; Dr. Josephine Harris proves herself to be an ideal collaborator; and one of the many reasons, she has earned an outstanding respect, from those she serves.

Dr. Harris' mantra is simple: She is inherently committed to the emboldening of women, particularly military spouses; facilitating for them all, an opportunity of hope. Whether it be through transformational messages of professional and/or personal growth, Dr. Harris was born, to encourage, motivate, and empower women of all cultures.

Dr. Josephine Harris backs an amazing portfolio, with an incredible regard for higher learning. She has attained a Ph.D. in Psychology, Post-Master Online Teaching Psychology Certificate, a Master of Philosophy in Psychology, M.S. in Psychology, and a B.S. in Criminal Justice Administration. She is certified in both, Teaching English to Speakers of Other Languages (TESOL) and Teaching English as a Foreign Language (TEFL) and is an Internationally Licensed Psychotherapist, proudly serving the Seoul Counseling Center in South Korea, since 2018.

Naturally, Dr. Josephine Harris has served as a staple in both, the professional vernacular of mental health advocacy, as well as several other philanthropic driven platforms. She is a Member of the Board of Directors at SafePlace Olympia, which advocates for survivors of both sexual assault and domestic violence, Delta Sigma Theta Sorority, Psi Chi Member; the NAMI Association, CHADD Association, CHADD International, American Psychology Association, American Counseling Association, Addiction Counseling Association, Phi Sigma Theta National Society; and the Applied Behavior Association.

Though recognized on various platforms for her outstanding abilities, Dr. Harris considers her greatest accomplishment to have been her contributions as the International Coordinator for Seoul, South Korea, where she developed and implemented the Applied Behavioral Analysis services (ABA) program; receiving more than 90% positive post-program evaluations, while having also developed instructional coaching materials and facilitated clients, with mental health illness. Dr. Harris also managed to develop and present the Adverse Childhood Experiences (ACEs) program related trauma/stress within the military community.

Dr. Harris' philanthropy is inspired by a famous quote from the late Maya Angelou, that states:

"I've learned that people will forget what you said, people will forget what you did, but people will never forget how you made them feel.

When Dr. Harris is not out advocating for those in need, she is a deeply appreciated member of her communal body, and loved greatly, by family and friends.

Dr. Josephine Harris. | Visionary. | Advocate. | Servant Leader.
Facebook: www.facebook.com/DrJoHarris
LinkedIn: www.linkedin.com/in/dr-josephine-harris

The Beauty of a Breakthrough
"I am the rose that grew from a crack in the concrete."

by Jill Hunter

*A*wakened by the loud buzzing of my alarm clock, startled by that annoying noise that wakes me up every morning for work at 6:00 o'clock am. After pushing the snooze button, a couple of times to get a few more minutes of shut eye, I stretch my arms up to the ceiling, thanking God for allowing me to see another day. I was a twenty-four-year-old mother of two boys, ages three and six, trying to figure out my journey in life living with my mother at the time.

As I started my every morning routine, getting my boys ready for daycare and myself dressed for work, which is a well-programmed task that I perform as a single mother.

I had just made the ultimate decision to finally break it off with my toxic narcissistic boyfriend. We had been dating for almost a year, and our relationship was on and off like a light switch, with most of our arguments starting because I would find out about all the other girls that he had been cheating on me with.

At this point in time of my life, I was a certified "people pleaser." I worried about what others said and thought about me. I always wanted to fit in. I lived my life in the shadows of other people. I lived in fear, bondage, and my own insecurities of not being good enough, smart enough, or beautiful enough. I was always pointing out my flaws and inadequacies. I am talking, low self-esteem at its finest. I didn't know who I was, I didn't know my worth, and I didn't know where I was going. I was always taught to treat people the way I wanted to be treated. But in the real world, those are the people that are considered "green" or weak, the ones getting used and mistreated.

However, as time progressed, things between us started to get serious. I noticed then he started being more controlling, overprotective, and possessive. Next thing I knew, we were moving into a one-bedroom apartment together. I remember one night as I was in bed sleeping when my phone rang it was my friend, she said: "Jill, get your ass outta that bed, I see your man and his baby mama in a car together, I am coming to pick you up, so you can see for yourself!" She picked me up, we drove by, and there he was in the car with the mother of his first son. My feelings were hurt. For the first time, I had seen him with my own eyes. I went back home, laid in bed, and cried a river of tears. Pretending as if I were asleep, I waited and waited for him to come home.

He finally made it; I heard the key in the door, the doorknob turns, and every footstep he took. That night I had already made up in my mind that I was leaving him for good. The next morning after he left, I started packing, leaving him my exit message: I wrote on the dresser mirror with black cherry lipstick that read, "YOU CAN HAVE HER WITH YOUR BROKE ASS!"

The next day I went to get the rest of my things. All the furniture had been destroyed; there was shattered glass all over the living room floor. It looked as if he had taken a vase and just slammed it directly into the center of the glass coffee table. He destroyed the entertainment center and shattered my dresser mirror. Everything that I left was destroyed.

He didn't take the break-up well at all; he was angry. Oh, he was big mad.

One morning I was on my way to take my boys to Merry-Go-Round Kindergarten. I saw his dark Gray Chevy Caprice creeping on the next street over., looking through my peripheral vision from my rearview mirror as I was backing out of the driveway at my mom's house, I made sure that my boys were buckled up tightly and secure in the back seat. As I was running into the daycare, I felt a swift wind behind me, and I thought, 'no, he didn't just follow me into this daycare.' Before I knew it, he had pulled me by my ponytail onto the floor and started kicking me in my back as the children and teachers watched in shock. I couldn't believe this was happening to me. The owner of the daycare immediately called the police and filed a report. He kept calling me, and I refused to answer his calls. I was going to show him that I was serious this time. I was done, and there was nothing he could say or do to get me back.

The next morning, I decided to drive my mother's gold Toyota 4 runner Sports Utility Vehicle. As I was heading to work, my phone kept ringing. After the sixth time, I looked at the caller ID and answered angrily, "what do you want?"

He said, "My family is going to be sad, and your family is going to be sad."

I said, "Man, whatever!" that is my favorite line to say when I don't give a damn.

I hung up the phone, turned the music up loud, and proceeded to my destination, which was work. I got off the ramp, merged left onto Hwy 57 to turn right into the SunPlex Industrial Park, and as soon as I turned left, I felt a hard hit and heard a loud BOOM. He had struck my head on in his Chevy Caprice, and the airbag deployed and hit me in the face; I could smell the scent of burnt rubber in the air. Then he jumped out of his car like a mad man holding a TEC-9 automatic version of a military machine gun. This gun could empty a 32-round magazine, and he had a gun that could be used against five to ten individuals in minutes. I saw my life flash before my eyes for a split second; I saw a bullet through the windshield, and blood splattered everywhere. I had to think of something quickly; the first words that came to my mind that saved my life that day was "I LOVE YOU, I WILL BE WITH YOU!" I shouted loud and clear twice.

He immediately lowered the gun, came over to the driver's side window where I was, and leaned in to kiss me; his face had this look like something had taken over his body. I could see it all over his face, and his lips felt cold as ice.

I was in a state of shock. He proceeded to get into the vehicle with me; he said, "Let's just leave" I nodded, I looked at him, keeping my eyes on that gun, I pushed the airbag down and slowly began to move around his car to move forward. By the time we were about 50 feet from the area of the accident. The police arrived. They told him to step out of the vehicle, and on that day, he went to jail, charged with kidnapping and assault.

Nevertheless, I had to go to the emergency room, and I was shaking with nervousness! I was traumatized! After the investigation, the police told me that there was a suicide letter in his car's trunk; he had planned to kill me and then kill himself. But God saw fit for me to be here today to share my story with you. I thank God for my praying mother. My mother stayed on her knees, praying for her baby girl.

I felt victimized, confused, and lonely. In the midst of me trying to pick up the pieces of my broken heart, I found myself in the arms of another man in no time. Well, they say the best way to get over a man is to get under another one. Don't judge me; I know a lot of women and men who must have someone by their side because they don't feel complete by themselves. They have not mastered the art of Self Love. That is why it is very imperative to work on yourself before you rush into another relationship. I advise you to get to know YOU first, take time out for YOU. Love YOU first, then you can easily love another person effectively.

BE SELF FULL!

In all honesty, I didn't allow myself to heal; I did not take time out for self-care. I was still trying to figure out what my purpose here on earth was. Why did God spare me? Who was I? What is my worth?

The Beauty of a Breakthrough is that you can break a woman temporarily, but a real woman will always pick up the pieces, rebuild herself, and come back stronger than ever.

I SURVIVED!

I AM A SURVIVOR!

About Jill Hunter

Photographer: DP Photography, LLC

Jill Hunter is a native of Moss Point, MS. She is a serial entrepreneur and the mother of four. She is the CEO of Hunter Doll LLC, event coordinator, author, speaker, confidence & life coach, Yoni Health and Wellness Specialist. It is her desire to lead individuals to live a "Self-Full" life. Over the years, Jill has had many challenges and life struggles. The struggles began in her early childhood years. One of the initial challenges came with the fact of learning that she was adopted. After finding out this knowledge, Jill questioned who she was and her purpose in life. Due to this, she made countless bad decisions that resulted in domestic abuse, low self-esteem, abandonment, suicidal thoughts, multiple failed relationships and two marriages that both ended in divorce. During her cry for help, she became more self-care aware to become the best version of herself. Unapologetically, she is changing lives one by one hoping that one's self-esteem will no longer lack confidence but flourish into high heights, beyond measures. She encourages, uplifts, and brings positive energy that builds confidence in a world that sets limits and boundaries. Motto: "Why live empty, when you can live Self Full?"

Email- **jillhunterdoll@gmail.com**
Instagram - justjill94

Blazing My Own Path

by Kathy Knisley

I looked down the hallway and saw a face of an angel that had nothing but pure fear and terror in her little face because of what she was seeing. I can still only imagine how terrified she must have felt at that moment, watching her father strangle her mother. At that moment, I realized that I had done this for far too long. Not only did MY life hang in the balance at that moment, but I realized that I had also disregarded the well-being of my own two children. I am still not sure how I survived that night. I still find it odd that my only desire was to protect my children, even at that moment. It outweighed my need to protect myself.

How do I protect her from what she is seeing with her own eyes? How do I make what she is seeing go away? How do I continue to keep quiet, so I don't wake my kids? All of that passed through my head as he strangled me and told me that he was going to end me. I obviously survived. Everything that happened after that moment was not pleasant or easy. Frankly, at the time, it was harder to pull myself up and function than it was to let him choke the life out of me. I could have given in, but I did not!

This was not his first act of aggression, but as he would remind me later, he never actually hit me. While technically true, I found that there are so many other creative ways to physically and mentally hurt a person. The abuse didn't look like it did on TV; it was much more complicated. The words and demeaning comments were constant, but the physical attacks that he would explain away were far worse because I couldn't wrap my mind around it truly being abuse. After all, he wasn't actually "beating" me. My biases of what abuse looked like hindered my thought processes.

He had given me a black eye by throwing keys at my face, but he had me believing that I was just bad at catching things. He ripped the skin on my back, leaving me with a horrible scar; my thought process was it was an accident in the heat of an argument. I explained it all away, and he whole-heartedly supported the excuses I gave him. All of the abuse always came with apologies, and I would stay, time after time. I stayed with him for over five years through dating and marriage. I had come to believe that I was unable to survive without him with two kids in this world. He told me this so often I began to believe it.

What I failed to realize was the truth and reality of my life. I, too, was an active-duty military member, just like him. I had a good career and was making my way through the ranks. I was actually about to out-rank him and had been in for far shorter of a time. However, with each rank, he told me I didn't deserve it, I hadn't earned it, and that I hadn't been in long enough. I downplayed my successes; I wouldn't talk about the rank I made as I made them. It made my skin crawl because I completely believed that I didn't deserve it. In reality, I earned everything on my own. I had worked just as hard, if not harder than him. I was capable and able to support my family without him. When I finally realized all of that, the amount of strength I felt was overwhelming.

Why had I short-changed myself to stay with someone that did nothing but put me down in every aspect of life he could ever possibly think of? It was at this point that he lost his power and control over me. At that moment, I become my own everything, a constellation that was bound only by my two children. Allowing him to hold me down and rip my spirit from me was no longer an option. I wasn't raised to be this person, nor had I ever been this person before I met him. I was a trailblazer and a hell-raiser, and I did as I wanted, until him. I realized that this was not who I am. I am far too stubborn to give up or give in ever again from this point forward. No other person would ever dictate to me who or what I am. I blaze my own path.

Although I still struggle with why I stayed with him for almost five years, and why even after the divorce, I allowed him to stay in my life; I have grown to understand that the strength an abuser has over the abused is a power stronger than anyone could ever imagine unless they've been through it themselves. There is so much baggage that comes with the contemplation of why I stayed. I chose to focus on what mattered: my children. They are why I had to leave. They are why I couldn't give up. They are the only two people that have this much influence on the path I chose to blaze, that even in my weakest moments, they give me a strength that makes me dig deeper, work harder, and be better regardless of all the crap that is thrown at me.

Me focusing on my children got me back in school, and I finished two Associate's Degrees, one Bachelor's Degree, and finally, a Master's Degree. They gave me an understanding of life that allowed me to provide them with a life I never had, growing up in the streets of South Central Los Angeles. They gave me the drive and focus to experience my career progression that I never thought was possible. I was great at being a part of the military; I was great at relating to and leading others, and I was great at being a mother.

I grew to realize that I am a badass-boss-lady. I may have weak moments, but at my core, that is who I am. I've experienced trials and tribulations; that is just life. I remarried a man that supports and loves me in a way that I cannot fully comprehend. *My* children are *our* children. He raised the only children he has ever had as his own. We showed them what a healthy relationship looks like, what is acceptable for a woman to accept as treatment from any man, and how a young man should treat a woman. Although bio-dad has contact with them, we outweigh all of his dysfunction, and they have been allowed to make their own decisions on who we all are.

That angel face that saw her mother being strangled by her father that day in the hallway; the little girl I worried so much about how that moment would change her and possibly break her? She is now a successful college graduate in a healthy relationship with a great young man. She is far better and more defined as a young woman than I could have ever seen in that horrible moment. I can't say that everything we've been through since then hasn't impacted either of my kids or myself, but I can say that we blazed our path. We have become better for it and have not allowed a single event in our lives to dictate what our lives could have become.

About Kathy Knisley

Kathy Knisley is a coach, leader, and mentor in every aspect of her daily life. As an Active Duty service member and the Senior Enlisted Leader of a 600-person organization that supports 24,000 people she builds and grooms leaders every day. As a Chief Master Sergeant, she is a member of the vaunted top 1% of the world's greatest Air Force, leading her people through mission accomplishment daily.

She spends her spare time with her family and friends, traveling the world. She enjoys experiencing new cultures and experiences. When not traveling she invests her intellectual energy in learning more about the human condition.

Kathy holds a Bachelor's Degree in Business Management and Administration and a Master's Degree in Leadership and Coaching. In addition to both of those degrees she has accomplished over 1500 hours in counseling and 420 hours in instructing leadership courses.

Kathy has spent over 200 hours working in Fairfax County, Virginia's homeless community. She has also donated numerous hours raising money for Multiple Sclerosis research. Her accolades include being recognized as the 2020 Air Force Sustainment Center's Service Member with a Disability Award. Her husband, JJ and her two kids are the light of her life.

E-mail: <u>Kathy.knisley77@gmail.com</u>

Facebook: Kathy Knisley

Walking in My Truth

by Rianne Egana

There is a woman who seemingly had it all together. She lived in a beautiful house, raising a blended family and often traveling always on the move—a regular at social functions and sporting games. Leading an established career, she built. Now let me tell you about her dark secrets hidden behind the glamour and smiles. That woman is me; this is my story.

We dressed elegantly for the evening, complementing each other—a power couple attending a social event. However, my companion was agitated, distracted; thoughts crossed my mind being here before. My smile faded, preparing for the silent ride home. Sadness surfaced entering our house and knowing hurt always followed continuing in silence approaching my closet, looking at the door wearing its scar. It protected me as I retreated behind it. Clothes, shoes, purses, each bearing names from betrayal with other women. Praying in it was consistent.

Undressing revealing hidden bruises, I could no longer feel. My body was numb. A scarred smile no longer recognized. Years back, a tablet was smashed in my face because I answered his phone. In urgent care, several stitches were applied to close my lip. He tried to damage an internal smile that could never be broken.

Remembering my son's birthday months earlier, sensing then he was involved with someone. We had a horrific fight that day, right before leaving for our son's party. Withdrawn at the function, pretending it never happened. Thinking I deserved it, God, was I being punished? 1 Peter 4:16

The woman they think has it all together was losing herself and not understanding trauma bonds. In bed weeping silently so he wouldn't notice. This man I loved so dearly was becoming a stranger. Remembering times that I left and returned believing apologies saying to myself, "he never wanted to lose me." Renewing our vows eight months earlier, begging me, involving our pastor in marriage counseling. Only to now be put through another affair. Forgiving and then staying, I invested time, finances, sold my house, moving together. Counselors heard sessions about women he entertained becoming bullies. Some work meetings were with them at hotels during the day. All knew about me, some stalking me on social media, even sending friend requests. He wronged them, but hatred displayed towards me for his actions when busted. We discussed abuse, mental and physical. He convincingly wanted to do better. He was creating boundaries to save us. Realizing now one chooses to stay distracted, boundaries are problems for those uncommitted. Obviously, more time was being demanded of him, and I was in the way.

Sunday came, and he had another meeting. This time, I followed him. He picked up the woman he'd been seeing during the day. I was saddened to see his staff member. He had moved her and her children into an Airbnb. I was drained with no fight left. Tears didn't come when I asked him, "This who you've been seeing? How? You just had sex with me."

He called me crazy, telling her, "See, I told you she would make up things." I asked her why she was doing this, knowing he was married, but she didn't say two words. The level of disrespect displayed in front of her explained why they didn't respect his marriage. He left me standing on the street, shocked, and took her to dinner.

Embarrassed, I got tested for STDs. He'd still been intimate with me, believing him that there was nobody else. Breaking down on my knees and grabbing my Bible, I asked myself, "How could this happen again?"

I started praying for my husband; God spoke Jeremiah 14, *knowing he will visit them in their iniquity and sin.*

Friday, he picked a fight as an excuse to leave; I ran outside barefooted. After me, with rage, he was trying to break windows on the car to get me (often I wonder if I would be here today had he been successful in breaking the glass). Shortly after, he departed to celebrate her birthday. What he was willing to commit to being with his mistress minutes later alerted me to leave.

Taking our son, I drove nowhere to go. I was ashamed of losing myself. Seeing his calls, he was looking for us leaving her party; I didn't answer. I prayed, reading Psalm 55 describing my cries to God so vividly. Why didn't he just end the relationship with me? The one I was in covenant with betrayed me.

Confused women fix women's crowns, but you have women helping destroy relationships, backstabbing, mess with married men, and hurting children who become silent victims in broken homes—adding to statistics already damaging our youth. Realizing these types of women didn't care just there for benefits, gaining stolen moments. Images manipulate us. A lifestyle not seeing I made our home good but in the midst of spiritual warfare.

He flew out of town with her, intentionally posted on social media. She even put on glasses I had worn with no shame. Moving with just our clothes, the locks were changed the following day. Welcoming her into our house among belongings built for years. Not understanding what kind of woman and mother herself would do something like that. He had her driving our cars, his revenge of "how dare you leave me." He wasn't leaving his wife wanting to play both sides. I showed her messages of truth even though I shouldn't explain marriage. She didn't care.

Nurturing our sons hurt and feelings of abandonment. He woke up in nightmares thinking he would lose me too. My children and I were discarded. Shut out by people around often. My ex displayed behavior condoned like soap operas, the wife replaced by mistresses overnight like I no longer existed. Regardless of lies told, nobody could erase the facts he was married.

I Questioned God shameful of me, revealing Psalm 73 becoming that beast in front of him envious, hurt, yes, every right to be angry. It was in those moments of tears looking down my legs were no longer bruised; my arms hadn't felt pain for months.

Losing everything at 18, I faced homelessness before. Again, for Hurricane Katrina. Knowing struggle losing everything a third time was different this time in betrayal. Attempts to even financially bully me even though always having my own. He didn't care where our son slept while making sure the mistress and her kids had a roof—expecting me to just get over it and disappear. God prepared me. No longer angry at women, my ex bonded in sin with their selfish motives. Isaiah 3: 8-26 Revelation 2: 18-29. By December, she became discarded herself; did she think it wouldn't happen to her?

During separation, seven additional women entered our home. Matthew 12:45. The teacher that met him at hotels triggering counseling. Another his oldest child's mother. Facing mixed emotions. This person obsessively harassed and stalked me for years, leaving the children traumatized. There is a difference between hurt people hurting people and straight malice. Unspeakable things she did in bondage a soul tie he brought home. Proving that drama would've never ended. He Intentionally stood distracted. God revealed, providing me peace and finally closing that chapter.

Don't get angry at the women that interfere in relationships, desperate seeking their own. You didn't marry them. A man protects his home. Jezebel Spirit is explained throughout the Bible I saw in them. Forgiving the women praying they change their wicked ways. I Forgave him too.

I'm walking in my truth, no more shame replaced with healing. Seeking forgiveness from my children who suffered from no fault of their own. Wanting them to know it's not okay what they witnessed. Nobody deserves that treatment. Society shames us from speaking about this while these behaviors are condoned. Many don't say anything because they don't want judgment or friends upset with them. Noticing often women spend so much time fixing the man that already showed doesn't care. We stop recognizing ourselves as the victim. It ultimately enables their behavior.

God provided a small apartment, giving up everything I had, knowing otherwise I would've still been there, watching everything unfold. Learning not everyone checking on you has the right intentions. Countless nights unable to sleep or awakened early mornings. I started taking that time to pray to listen to God's messages. Through my worst tears, he provided. Every time I grew angry, he reassured revealing answers.

Witnessing him moving in my son's life. Spiritually healing knowledge, my son displayed direct messages from God. He's simply grateful.

He was realigning me from people that were there to just have seats at the table and replacing them with God-fearing survivors. Rejoicing in his grace speaking of his greatness, I'm blessed Psalm 105. I fixed my relationship with God. The favor is shown for staying faithful, patient, and trusting. I have my life. God answered, now providing a beautiful home. Romans 8:28 New beginnings. My children never have to worry again about where they'll sleep.

This happens in every walk of life; without discrimination, someone suffers silently. More women need to come together from a place of godliness to empower others. Praying for strength. Being kind as we become light someone needs right on time. Providing reassurance all will be well getting out sooner, there is life after. I continue to uplift marriages where both partners are willing to work on it. And to also hope the abusers and adulterers turn to God. I'm living witness to God's change in people. Addictions and habits were erased overnight, even after 25+ years of struggle. Turning pain into purpose. This is me walking past my hell.

About Rianne Egana

Rianne Egana is an accomplished Assistant Vice President Relationship Manager. Currently living in New Orleans, Louisiana.

Her 25+ years of extensive financial consulting background has helped countless small business owners and entrepreneurs with business growth, and success expanding their opportunities. Her passion for traveling traces back to years spend abroad. Growing up in the Netherlands raised fluent in Dutch. From there living in Belgium part of a unique military brat family. Attending S.H.A.P.E American High School.

Being bi-racial she embraces learning about different cultures educating herself along the way. Getting excited about growth in individuals and herself alike. Stemming from her drive and willingness always helping others. She's currently working on her next upcoming project to launch Blessings 2 Blessings Waymaker a program she founded geared towards underprivileged and minority youth gain access to tutoring, life skills sessions, and motivational seminars helping with personal development and job preparation.

She was featured in Formidable Woman Magazine part of "Power 20" accomplished women in different industries and a Co-Author of "My Walk Past Hell" book anthology. She's taken studies back up at Tulane University.

She has 3 wonderful kids, 2 of whom have already graduated with great accomplishments of their own.

E-mail: B2BWaymaker@gmail.com

Website: www.b2bwaymaker.com

Please Come Out The Closet

by Jamillah Welch-Bercy

People in abusive relationships often attempt to leave their partners several times before they do. On average, someone who's in an abusive relationship will try seven times before leaving for good. I was one of those people. It was the year 2003 where I finally said ENOUGH! After a date night turned into me being physically, verbally abused, stung with a gun, and opening the closet door seeing our 11-year daughter crying, holding the phone because she'd just called 911. The look in her eyes crushed me. It was at that moment I knew I had to make a change. I didn't send him to jail that night; I lied to the police. A blind sense of loyalty, I guess.

Domestic violence at any age is wrong. The first time it happened to me, I was 15 years old.

May 1991 Newark NJ, backyard party the DJ playing Will Smith Summertime. I looked across the yard, and there he was, this brown-skinned, curly hair guy staring at me, smiling; he was cute, so I smiled back. He walked over we started talking. We connected instantly. The next few weeks, we saw each other every day, spoke on the phone every night. It was the start of teenage love.

That summer, I experienced a lot of first, including the first time he hit me. A boy from the neighborhood touched my leg and told me how pretty they were. Somehow word got back to him! When he finally saw me that day, he asked, "Did that nigga D touch your legs?" I looked at him nodding my head "yes." We argued; he then smacked me so hard my ear was ringing.

It felt like I was in the twilight zone. Did this boy just smack me? It took me a moment to process what had just happened; I was crying, hurt, and shocked. That was the day I should've told someone, walked away, and never looked back. However, I was no stranger to domestic violence, so I normalized it. I was young, in love, and he begged me to forgive him. "I will never hit you again he said," and I believe him.

As the summer months went by, our relationship was more potent than ever. We were inseparable, spending all those summer days and nights together sitting on the porch, listening to music. By September of that year, I had just turned sixteen and was starting to come into myself. Things changed fast. In mid-October, I found out I was pregnant. I was so scared I didn't know what to do. I remember thinking, "this can't be happening to me; I'm too young. I didn't even have sex that many times. My dad is going to kill me."

I finally found the courage to tell my parents, who were living in California at the time, this was a hard phone call for my mom, and I could hear the disappointment in her voice. And I'm sure she could hear the sadness and fear in mine.

I explained to her I didn't want to keep the baby. How was I going to take care of a baby? I was only 16. She understood, however having an abortion wasn't an option due to religious reasons. Hindsight, I couldn't imagine my life without her. After about a month or so, my mother was understanding. My father, however, didn't utter one word to me through my pregnancy. I felt hurt and sad; I knew he was disappointed.

Around my ninth month of pregnancy, I found myself homeless, couch surfing until one of my cousins let me stay with her for a few months. In July of 1992, I gave birth to a beautiful baby girl. She was my strength. She saved my life! After she was born, I still didn't have a steady place to live; I stayed with friends and family. Until I finally settled down at my daughter's great-grandmother's house (she was the grandmother of my daughter's father). That's when the mental and physical abuse started again. By this time, it wasn't just a slap. He was drinking more, and his attacks became too violent. He would come home about 2 in the morning demanding sex. One morning, I refused; he put a gun to my head and threatened to shoot me. I was so tired of him getting drunk coming home to terrorize me. I yelled, "DO IT, just do it! I'm fucking tired of this shit. Just kill me!"

I yelled this while I looked at my twelve-month-old daughter asleep in her bassinet. He smirked, put the gun up, and let me go back to bed. I remember his aunt, who lived downstairs, telling me, "just leave his ass."

A year later, he was in prison serving a four-year sentence for another crime. During that time, I decided I wasn't going to wait for him. It wasn't easy when he went to jail. I went through some trials and tribulations. His family asked me to move out, and I had nowhere to go; I'd hit rock bottom. A couple of years later, things began to look up. I had a good-paying job and was able to afford an apartment. I started dating, enjoying my life as any 21-year-old girl my age should do.

When he finally came home, I didn't immediately take him back. It took some time. He said prison changed him, and he wasn't the same person. He was saying all the right things. I wanted my family together so bad I decided to give it a chance. Well, prison *didn't* change him. A year and a half later, I found myself lying on the floor with him sitting on top of me, pinning my arms down and head butting me over and over again in the face. I ended up with a black eye, bruised face, and six stitches on my lip! I was ashamed and embarrassed when I went to work two days later; they didn't even recognize me. I told my manager and colleagues that I got jumped by a group of girls. They were so disturbed they had no choice but to send me home for over a week. This time I couldn't protect him because the person that took me to the hospital told them what happened, and the hospital called the police. They took my statement and pictures of my face said they would look for him and get back to me; however, that never happened! I guess a 22-year-old black girl from the hood wasn't important enough.

My family, however, was a different story. It was out I could no longer hide the bruises. My older boy cousins wanted to beat the shit out of him! I talked them out of it. I knew I would end up going back, and I did! Not only did I go back, but he also convinced me, and I convinced myself we could live together as a happy family. I was so naive and in love. So, I moved out of my place, and we moved in together.

Things were good for a while, but we always seemed to be at each other's throats. It was horrible if he was drinking or worse if we both were. We tried to make it work, but the fights were becoming more frequent and volatile. To the point, I thought he was going to kill me. We were fighting about him cheating again, and it ended up with me stomping his PlayStation, him throwing me on the bed, and strangling me.

I tried to fight back, but he was stronger than me; I was no match. I was gasping, telling him I couldn't breathe. He continued choking me. Out of my peripheral vision, I saw my purse lying on the bed. I knew I had a knife that I carried for protection. I reached inside, grabbed it, and stabbed him in the back. And just like that, he released me. Before I could even catch my breath, he started yelling, "you're going to jail!"

I was terrified. I watched the blood gush out of his back. I begged him not to call the police even though I was protecting myself. I thought we'd both end up in jail—neither of us reached out to the police because we didn't know what would happen to our daughter. I never thought she'd be the one to make the call in 2003 that saved me.

You see, the longer you live, the more mistakes you make. I promised myself that night I would never let any man put his hands on me. And I've kept that promise. I gave him a 30-day notice to leave since his name wasn't on the lease. I got help through counseling, hit the gym for some self-care, started traveling more, and never looked back. It wasn't a comfortable journey, but it was the one I had to take to get to where I am now. I've forgiven him for what he took me through, and we're cordial now for our daughter.

Today I'm happily married to a man that loves, respects, and protects me! Who kisses me on the forehead just to tell me how beautiful I am? A man who's asked me every single day since we've been together, "how did you sleep?"

Never give up and make peace with your past so it doesn't affect your present.

About Jamillah Welch-Bercy

The best trademark of successful entrepreneurship can be seen most prevalent through energized professionals who couple ambition with an unyielding sense of humanitarianism. Standing tall, amongst many, is the multifaceted business guru, Jamillah Welch-Bercy.

Jamillah Welch-Bercy is an author, investment specialist, philanthropist, and CEO and founder, of JW Investments LLC, where she specializes in the purchasing and renovation of homes in urban cities, repurposing them into suitable housing opportunities for low-income families. She is also co-founder of Texas Partners LLC, alongside her husband, specializing in acquiring homes, rehabbing, and selling them for profit. These property ventures are the fruits of Jamillah's audacity to reform her past, enhance the lives of urban communities, and walk into her life's purpose of compassionate entrepreneurship after surviving a mundane career in the telecommunications industry for over twelve years.

Jamillah's mantra is simple: she believes in "Never giving up, and always giving back."

True to her philanthropic nature, Jamillah has an annual relationship with volunteerism and often commits to facilitating communal drives and giveaways to those burdened by impoverished circumstances. Overcoming her traumatic past as a teenager, and often homeless mother, a survivor of domestic violence, Jamillah has made giving back a signature of the life she is determined to create not only for herself but for others. Her passion for this method of giving back is one of the many reasons Jamillah will soon launch **Nine18 House of Love, Inc**, a nonprofit organization concentrating on teenage mothers and young girls' shelter and safety.

Jamillah has made an exceptional lifestyle of outliving her past through her many business ventures and a genuine asset to various communities. In her free time, she enjoys traveling the world, assessing the vastness of creation, with a sincere gratitude for life. She loves cooking, dancing, stock trading, and spending time with loved ones. When she is not out changing the world, Jamillah is the hero at home, a loving wife, mother, aunt, and cherished friend.

Jamillah Welch-Bercy | Leader | Investor | Advocate.
Facebook: Jamillah Welch-Bercy
Email: hello@nine18houseoflove.org

Yea, Though I Walk Through the Valley of The Shadow of Death

by Dr. Miatta Hampton

May 4th, 2012, would be one of the hardest days I would ever have to face. My morning would be filled with mourning and would move faster than I would have anticipated. I don't cry at funerals, but that day I stood over my Uncle's casket and wept like a child. My mind could not fathom my loss. How could people, how could this world be so cold, so callous? As I stood over his casket, saying my final goodbye, I could hear him say, "no more, huh."

I had only been at work for about two hours. After rounding on my patients, I had just returned to the nurse's station when the nursing secretary informed me, I had a call waiting. "Who is it?" I asked.

She looked up and shrugged her shoulders and said, "it's a lady."

My mind immediately started racing. No one ever called me at work unless it was an emergency. What could this emergency be? I reached for the phone and said to myself, "Lord, don't let it be nothing crazy."

I hit the button that was holding the call, "this is Miatta."

"Hey, have you talked to grandma?" The voice on the other end asked. It was my niece inquiring about if I had spoken to my mom, her grandmother.

I replied, "No, why? What's up?"

The next thing that would come out of her mouth would drop my heart into the pit of my stomach. I talked to my mom, and she said, "Uncle Henry is dead." Wait, what? How does she know? Who told her that?

James "Henry" Sando Madave Cooke, my guy, my favorite Uncle, was born in Liberia in 1957 and immigrated to the United States of America in 1988. He would give you the shirt off his back. My guy was gone, and he was not coming back. I hung up the phone with my niece and told the other nurse on the floor to watch my patients; I need to take a break and make a phone call. I left the floor and headed to the elevator. Trying not to panic, I paced, wondering why it was taking the elevator so long. I got on the elevator and pressed "2," which was the floor the crosswalk was on and could provide me with the most privacy I needed. Finally, at the crosswalk, I called my mom, and when she answered, I could hear the distress in her voice.

"Mom, I just got a call about Uncle Henry; what's the deal?"

She answered, "We are at the police station waiting for someone to come and talk to us. No one will tell us anything; all we know is he got stopped last night in a routine traffic stop for speeding, and they killed him."

I replied, "Huh, who is they? Are you sure they have the right person? I mean, what happened?"

She answered, "I don't know, but I think it is true; your brother said he found his phone on the coffee table this morning, and he doesn't go anywhere without his phone."

I braced myself for the worst. I got off the phone and was headed back to my unit. My throat hurt, I had a lump in it, and my eyes begin to fill. I just want to know what happened. I did not understand. As I made my way back into the nurse's station, I made eye contact with a peer; she asked was everything ok. I explained to her that my Uncle was stopped for speeding and something went wrong because now he was dead. I attempted to continue to work and keep a level head as I had patients to take care of, medication to administer, dressing to change, so I put on a poker face, rolled my sleeves up, and continued to work.

As the day went on, I had this intense feeling of fear, a discomfort in my chest that had never been there before. My heart was skipping beats, and I was frequently feeling like my throat was going to close and I was going to die. There was a visiting cardiac nurse on the unit that day, and she listened to my heart and informed me I was having heart arrhythmias or palpitations, and she was going to call the cardiologist to get me seen that day. I went to see the cardiologist that day and walk out of his office wearing a 30-day heart monitor. I was experiencing panic attacks brought on by stress, the stress of losing a loved one suddenly and tragically with no answers as to what happened or why.

The following day I had a conversation with my dad concerning the circumstances surrounding Uncle Henry's death, and there were a lot of things in question. The newspaper did not hesitate to write an article that painted him in a bad light. What did they mean he was resisting arrest and attempting to flee? Something did not sound right. I reached out to Mr. Jordan Quinn, the contributor of the article, and asked whether there was a dash camera video, and pointed out he had been placed in a Safe Wrap. According to the manufacturer's guidelines, the device was inappropriately used. I was angry and encouraged my dad to get an independent autopsy and not to go with the San Joaquin County Corner's cause of death. It would take a few days to get the autopsy performed and get the report, and the anticipation of what would be found made my stress worse, and I continued to have panic attacks multiple times throughout the day. I had to suffer in silence because I felt I was the strong one, and I needed to hold it together for my family. I had to be able to explain the independent autopsy report, and if I allowed these panic attacks to get the best of me, then I could not be there for my family. So, I suppressed my emotions and hid the attacks from my family.

Finally, the autopsy report came in, and it would be the beginning of my trauma and recurrent anxiety. I could not believe what I was reading, "death undetermined." How is that possible. As I read through the report, I discovered my Uncle suffered a skull fracture, subdural hematoma, right orbital bone collapsed, petechial hemorrhaging, missing vital organs, missing tongue, throat muscle, missing rib cage, and spinal cord. The Stockton Police Department took his life, and the San Joaquin County Coroner's office defiled his corpse. It was a cover-up, and there was nothing we could do to prove it.

I had to figure out how to cope; I had a husband and children who needed me. I did not want to take anxiety medication, so I relied heavily on my relationship with God. As hurtful and traumatic as this was, I had to believe it was for my good and that things would ultimately work out. I committed Philippians 4:6-8 to my memory. ***"Be anxious for nothing, but in everything by prayer and supplication, with thanksgiving, let your requests be made known to God; and the peace of God, which surpasses all understanding, will guard your hearts and minds through Christ Jesus. Finally, brethren, whatever things are true, whatever things are noble, whatever things are just, whatever things are pure, whatever things are lovely, whatever things are of good report, if there is any virtue and if there is anything praiseworthy—meditate on these things.***

Reading scripture, prayer, journaling, self-care, being careful not to internalize my feelings, and relaxation techniques such as deep breathing are things that I used to manage my anxiety. In 2017, world-renowned CTE doctor Bennet Omalu resigned as the Medical Examiner in San Joaquin County, alleging Corner Steve Moore tried to influence medical findings during autopsy's that involved law enforcement officers.

The realization that we are subject to death often comes through illness, suffering, deprivation, and oppression. But God can lead us through these dark times. The earth is the Lord's and everything that dwells in it. Although we go through trials and tribulations, we can trust and rely on God to bring us through. Even though I walked through the valley of the shadow of death, I refused to let unforgiveness reside in my heart. I may not ever understand why my Uncle had to succumb to such a fate, but I know that it is a part of all the things working for my good.

About Dr. Miatta Hampton

Dr. Miatta Hampton is a Nurse Practitioner and Nursing Leader. She impacts others with her powerful, relatable messages of pursing purpose and learning to lead where you are. She coaches and inspires mompreneurs to create balance, culture, and growth, personally, professionally, and financially. Dr Miatta is a speaker, coach, author, and entrepreneur who empowers her audience to live life on purpose and according to their dreams.

Dr. Miatta Hampton is the CEO and founder of Washroom Devotions LLC. She coaches women to turn their purpose into profit and how to profit in adversity. She has served as a guest speaker and panelist for Success Women's Conference, Dr. Trenese McNealy Virtual Summit and Born 2 Danz Worship Arts Conference. She has served as a contributor to Sheology.com blog.

Dr. Miatta hold a Bachelor's of Arts Degree from Fisk University, bachelor of Nursing from Belmont University, Master's of Science in Nursing from Tennessee State University with a concentration in

Family Nurse Practitioner, Post Master's Certificate in Nursing Education from Tennessee State University and a Doctorate of Nursing Practice from Purdue University. She is a wife to Latrae Hampton and a mother to four beautiful girls ages 17, 12, 7 and 2.

E-mail: miattahampton@gmail.com
Instagram: drmiattahampton

Bent, Not Broken

by Lee Mariano

Have you ever felt so low that you didn't think you could lift yourself off of the ground?

That was me twenty-six years ago. I was the woman who'd fallen into the trap of marrying someone who communicated using his fists. Who used vicious words to break me down and crush my soul. A husband who cheated with other women, flaunting his behavior in my face. If I challenged him, he shut me up with anger and the force of his fists.

If you met me today, you may be shocked to hear my story. You may ask how I could have been in an abusive relationship. To the casual observer, I have a successful life. I succeeded in my career and achieved that coveted C-suite title. I'm an Amazon and a USA Today Bestselling Author, and my home life is happy and blessed. But, if I'm so confident, successful, creative, and strong, how did I end up with a man who abused me?

The truth?

I struggled for years with my own feelings of inadequacy. I compared myself to others and always found myself lacking. This feeling wasn't new to me. It didn't happen overnight. This was an ongoing feeling that I'd had since I was a young girl.

"Your face is long. You look like a horse."

"Your hair is nappy. You should straighten it."

"How come you're so big? Stop eating so much."

"You're not as cute as your friends, but you're alright."

Statements like that impacted how I thought about myself and how I viewed the world. My behaviors manifested in how I strived for acceptance, how I stayed close to people who didn't treat me with love, and how I looked for love from men who were no good for me.

My ex-husband was the guy all the women wanted, and he knew it. When I met him, I was a single mother with a one-year-old son. He bought him shoes, played with him, and accepted him as his own son. Looking back now, I realize just how stupid and naïve I truly was.

The signs were there, but I was so blinded by my delusion of finally finding my Prince Charming, that I chose to ignore what was happening. Maybe it was because I'd seen domestic violence in my family. My perspective of life and relationships and acceptable behavior was skewed. It allowed me to accept the things he did to me. I didn't want to be the woman who let this "good man" walk away. I was under the misguided perception that if I left, I would be judged and ridiculed for leaving. In reality, I stayed because I thought that was what I was supposed to do.

The first time he was violent happened less than two months after we were married. It was an argument that started after I confronted him about a woman in his life that I was uncomfortable with. A woman who I couldn't help but compare myself to and the feelings of "lack" came roaring back. There was something in the way he spoke to her, the way she always came over to our home looking for him, the way they had private conversations that no one else could hear.

One thing to remember is that during this time, I was a United States Marine. Someone who should be strong and independent and powerful. But with him, everything I thought I was, flew out the window. As did my pride and my self-worth. His anger was palpable. He couldn't believe I dared question him. Why couldn't I just shut up about it? Why did I always have to ruin things? Why was I so stupid?

As he said these words, my heart broke. He didn't love me. He didn't view me as a woman to protect and cherish. No matter what vows he'd taken in front of God and all our witnesses. My body curled into itself and the tears started to flow. But seeing my hurt didn't make him reconsider what his words were doing to me. No, it only escalated his anger.

That's when he threw his large drink in my face as we were driving on-base so he could drop me off at work. I still remember the cold liquid and ice hitting my skin. I can remember the way he looked at me as if I meant nothing to him, and the venom he spewed as he yelled at me to leave him alone and stop talking about things I knew nothing about.

Yet, in my shock, when he pulled up to my work location, I got out and walked inside the building. Soda dripping from my hair and staining my clothing. I later found out that the people around me knew what was happening to me but chose to stay silent. They didn't want to get involved in a private situation between a wife and husband.

The black eyes I tried to cover with make-up were still visible. The busted lips I tried to hide with lipstick or by shielding my face were still noticeable to those around me. I deluded myself. None of this was hidden, they just didn't know how to help. But one night, about a year after we married, all the questions about how others could help went out the window.

By this time, his affair with the other woman had been confirmed. He'd forced himself on me while punching me in the face because I didn't want to be intimate. His assaults on me had become common, to the point that I became a recluse, only going to work and then back home to take care of my son. I was embarrassed. I was ashamed. I couldn't share my pain with anyone else.

My son had just turned two-years-old, and he didn't realize what was happening. All he knew, was that his mommy was being hurt. His love for me outweighed his own sense of safety. That night, my ex-husband was angry with me again because I confronted him about his mistress. He'd taken her to visit his mother, which was the final straw. Not the physical or verbal abuse, but my embarrassment that he'd taken his mistress to meet his mother.

But I'd decided to leave, which is what I told him that night when he came home. If you know anything about abusers, then you know it's the power and control they crave. To take that control away from them, to make them feel as if they've lost the power they have over you, is what can take their anger from zero to sixty in less than a second.

Not only did he get a knife from our kitchen and chase me around the house threatening to kill me, but he also did this in front of my young child. I begged him not to hurt me. Tears flowed down my face as I tried to tell my baby to go back to his room, to not get involved. I cowered on the floor as he punched me repeatedly, telling me how useless I was. How he wished he'd never married me and that his mother told him not to marry me because I was so ugly. The entire time, I pleaded with him to just let me walk away, that I would leave and never come back. Whether he became tired, or my pleading got through to him, he stopped beating on me and left the house.

Hurt and scared, the first thing I did was grab my child and hug him close to me. Then I picked up the phone and called 9-1-1. No longer would I serve as his punching bag. I would never again allow myself to be put in this situation or allow my son to see a man beat on his mommy. No matter what environment I'd grown up in, or the negative beliefs I had about myself, I would never again be that woman.

Not everyone can escape their abuser. Not everyone has the opportunity to reinvent themselves. But the one thing to remember is that you can build a different life for yourself. How I survived, I will never know. But I knew I needed to live a different life for myself and my son.

My story is painful, but I've learned what I can accomplish when I silence the negative thoughts, focus on my growth, and hold my head high because I'm confident in the woman I've become. I've fought through my own Hell on several occasions, and I've risen from the ashes like a phoenix rising. I've built a life I can be proud of and I share my story to help someone else who may be struggling to find their way to the other side.

If I can do it, I know you can as well. You just need to have faith in yourself and believe that you can step into your power and reclaim your life.

About Lee Mariano

The possibility of transforming lives is not attained, without compassionate leaders, committed to an unyielding gift, of inspiring others. Championing that principle with exceptional grace; is the dynamic life enthusiast, Lee Mariano.

Lee Mariano is an author, speaker, business guru, and CEO and founder of **Alexidom Coaching**; a multifaceted coaching specialty centered around helping clients to increase their self-confidence, reclaim their personal power, and rediscover their identity, so that they can successfully achieve their goals; and attain the life they desire most. Reputed for her impressive 23-year career as a C-Suite Executive and Senior Leader, Lee proves her tenure in people management and career coaching to be quintessential; equipping her with the dedication and insight needed, to help clients transform their very own lives.

Lee Mariano's mantra is simple: Show up with confidence. Speak with authority, and get things done.

Lee merges an ability to help others, with a deep sentiment for education, authorship, advocacy, and communal service. She holds a bachelor's degree in business management and has served her country as a US Marine Corps Veteran. She is also a USA Bestselling Author and champions domestic violence advocacy; as she herself, is a proud survivor. Lee uses her experiences as a survivor to influence women to reinvent themselves, speak their personal truth, and begin again; some of the many attributes she offers through her coaching practice. Her intention is clear: Lee wants women to stop hiding behind the labels that others have placed on them, and to remain resolved to their purpose and the possibility of creating their own future.

When Lee is not out helping to empower women through **Alexidom Coaching,** she is a beloved member of her chosen community, a cherished mother, and friend.

Lee Mariano. | Speaker. | Advocate. | Guru.
Website: https://alexidomcoach.com
Email: alexidomcoach@gmail.com

The Thorn in My Flesh – Uterine Fibroids

by Cynthia E. Fields

"And lest I should be exalted above measure through the abundance of the revelations, there was given to me a thorn in the flesh, the messenger of Satan to buffet me, lest I should be exalted above measure." ~ 2 Corinthians 12:7

*I*n less than a year, I underwent two surgeries to treat uterine fibroids. The months prior, my symptoms left me feeling physically and mentally exhausted. At the time of my surgery, my uterus had grown to be two inches above my belly button; a normal uterus is located below the belly button. A healthy uterus is the size of a pear; my biggest fibroid was the size of a lemon. Nagging pain in my pelvis plagued me daily. Surgery became the only answer, and I had two options: 1) hysterectomy or 2) abdominal myomectomy; I chose the latter, a procedure that removes each tumor individually.

After the first surgery, my doctor handed me a photo of what looked like globs of fat covered in blood; those were my fibroids. I asked, "How many were there?"

She responded, "I stopped counting after 25."

I sat in shock and disbelief. Days later, I lay in bed recovering at home, feeling a sense of relief, falsely believing that my journey of terror was over. Little did I know that a second surgery was just ten months away.

My battle with fibroids began almost a decade before the war finally ended. A few small blood clots appeared during my monthly cycle, sparked curiosity. A few short years later, the situation progressed to include heavy bleeding. My solution was to shift from regular pads to super pads. Then came a defining moment during graduate school. Sitting in my Saturday class, a momentary shift in my wooden chair resulted in blood spilling over my pad. Slowly closing my eyes, I released a deep sigh, and thought "Oh no."

I sat in an anxious panic, waiting for class to end. Once the room cleared, I stood slowly and spotted a huge smear of blood on the chair. After the cleanup, I exited campus, jacket tied around my waist, feeling confused and embarrassed. I asked myself, "How is this happening to a grown woman?"

Plagued with concern, I scheduled an exam with my Gynecologist. An ultrasound followed, along with confirmation that I had fibroid tumors. Fear engulfed me because "tumors" could only mean cancer, right? Next came the news that they were not cancerous and that I would be treated with birth control pills to regulate the flow and decrease the amount of bleeding. I was content with the treatment plan, but it only worked for a few years before my symptoms worsened.

My blood clots grew from penny-sized to golf-ball-sized. I moved from regular pads to extra heavy overnight pads with wings. I lived in constant fear of period-related accidents. My tote bag was overflowing with panty liners, tampons, pads, ibuprofen, and wipes. The next defining moment occurred as I was leading a professional workshop in front of a crowd of 50 people. In the midst of speaking, I felt blood streaming down both my legs. Panic swept over me as I envisioned red stains seeping through my taupe-colored pantsuit...thank God it didn't. My 4-hour drive home required five bathroom stops to manage the flow.

Another time I was riding a commuter train home when blood transferred onto my pants; thank God I was wearing a long black coat. After hastily cleaning up in the station's nasty bathroom, I misplaced my train ticket. Looking disheveled and on the verge of tears, I approached the station attendant in exhaustion, "I lost my ticket."

With a look of compassion, she softly responded, "You did?" and motioned towards the exit gate for me to leave. I concluded that she was an angel in disguise because normal circumstances would have required me to pay an additional fare. I silently prayed, "Thank you, Jesus".

The scariest blow happened when I blacked out and saw stars as I walked from my front door to the family room. Thankfully I recovered before hitting the floor. A subsequent doctor's visit diagnosed me with severe anemia, which explained my inability to walk up our first flight of 7 stairs at home without feeling weak and winded. I ended up going to the ER and received two pints of blood.

During the final stages before surgery, my periods were occurring every 2 ½ - 3 weeks. My quality of life was shattered. The bleeding and blood clots became so ferocious that I was visiting the bathroom every hour to relieve myself. Each visit filled the toilet with burgundy water so dark that the bottom was invisible. It became typical for me to walk from my bed to the bathroom, crouched over, holding up my pad to prevent blood from escaping. One particular bathroom visit revealed a pad holding a heaping mound of tiny individual blood clots that looked like bits of liver. I gagged in disgust. Depression set in, and tears flowed as I processed what I just experienced. At that moment, I realized that I was experiencing my version of Hell on earth.

I became reliant upon FMLA (Family Medical Leave Act) leave in order to protect my job. Each month I was calling in sick for at least three days. My frequent absences resulted in worry that I was sabotaging my career. Social invitations were denied, and I began to feel depressed and isolated. Then the pity parties began. My constant questions to God: "Why is this happening to me?" "What did I do to deserve this?" I concluded that fornication was to blame. Surely this was punishment for sex outside of marriage. Afterall, Hebrew 4:16 states, *"Be not deceived; God is not mocked: for whatsoever a man soweth, that shall he also reap."* I used that scripture to condemn myself repetitively.

Mark 5:25-34 speaks about the woman who had an issue of blood for 12 years. *Verse 26 states, "And had suffered many things of many physicians, and had spent all that she had, and was nothing bettered, but rather grew*

worse", I felt like that woman. Since I knew of no one else suffering like me, I believed Satan's lies that I was a freak. Afraid of judgment, I kept my sickness to myself and chose to suffer in silence.

After finally deciding upon surgery that resulted in a normal cycle flow, I felt excited and relieved. But that excitement was short-lived when the heavy bleeding returned four months later. The cause, a substantially sized fibroid that could not be removed during the initial surgery due to its close proximity to a blood vessel; removing it could have led to an emergency

Hysterectomy. A second surgery was imminent, but with it came long-term relief. Praise God!

Lessons learned through my painful journey:

- **Christ suffered, so we must also suffer** - Suffering is guaranteed as we draw closer to God, and we may not be the cause. *"For even hereunto were ye called: because Christ also suffered for us, leaving us an example, that ye should follow his steps: Who did not sin, neither was guile found in his mouth: Who, when he was reviled, reviled not again; when he suffered, he threatened not; but committed himself to him that judgeth righteously:" 1 Peter 2:21-23*

- **Don't suffer in silence** - God did not intend for us to suffer alone. Confide in a trusted friend and/or family member. *"Bear ye one another's burdens, and so fulfil the law of Christ." Galatians 6:2*

- **The importance of Compassion** - The transit worker taught me not to label someone based on one interaction; you don't know what they experienced right before meeting you. *"Put on therefore, as the elect of God, holy and beloved, bowels of mercies, kindness, humbleness of mind, meekness, longsuffering;" Colossians 3:12*

- **You're not the only one** - While the circumstances may be different, God promises that you are not the first in your situation. *"The thing that hath been, it is that which shall be and that which is done is that which shall be done: and there is no new thing under the sun." Ecclesiastes 1:9*

- **Don't believe Satan's lies** - Negative self-talk is a weapon of the Devil. *"When he speaketh a lie, he speaketh of his own: for he is a liar, and the father of it." John 8:44*

- **Suffering does not last forever -** This too shall pass. *"For our light affliction, which is but for a moment, worketh for us a far more exceeding and eternal weight of glory;" 2 Corinthians 4:17*

- **Persevere in prayer** - Cry out to God for help. *"Let us therefore come boldly unto the throne of grace, that we may obtain mercy, and find grace to help in time of need." Hebrews 4:16*

- **Trials are designed to mature us** - Growing pains strengthen us. *"But the God of all grace, who hath called us unto his eternal glory by Christ Jesus, after that ye have suffered a while, make you perfect, stablish, strengthen, settle you." 1 Peter 5:10*

- **God will deliver -** Don't give up! *"...weeping may endure for a night but joy cometh in the morning." Proverbs 30:5*

About Cynthia E. Fields

Cynthia E. Fields is an author, organizational strategist, certified coach, and an exemplary leader, with a quintessential vernacular for achieving high results through organizational leadership. Cynthia is reputed for her innate ability for filling lines of business, where the undertaking would be seemingly impossible to accomplish, and enhancing them into outstanding collateral successes. Bringing over 15 years of professional experience in Human Resource Management, Cynthia knows the importance of performance management, culture enhancement, and employee engagement. Cynthia is soon planning to merge those traits with her overall life's purpose; inspiring and encouraging others, especially disadvantaged youth and women clientele.

Cynthia holds a Master of Organization Development from Pepperdine University, which facilitated opportunities for international studies in France, Costa Rica, and China; a Master of Public Administration (with honors) in Human Resources Management & Finance; and a Bachelor of Science degree in Business Administration and Marketing Management.

Cynthia is co-founder of Sisters Improving Self; a non-profit group for women aimed at professional, personal and spiritual development. She is a current mentor for High School girls in marginalized communities and is also a member of Alpha Kappa Alpha Sorority, Inc. and the Church of Christ.

Cynthia E. Fields. | Visionary. | Leader. | Advocate.

LinkedIn: https://www.linkedin.com/in/cynthia-e-fields

Clubhouse: @cynthiaefields

No More Locked Doors!

by Veronica McGee

Here I go again with another failed marriage and on my way to prison! I was on a downward spiral into the unknown, I didn't know If I was coming or going after my husband left me to be with another woman, but I never expected that I would be locked up.

I had gotten myself into trouble! Legal big trouble landed me in jail during the worst years of my life, and I was facing some time. I did not have a clue about Mississippi's judicial system at this point; what could be worse than my failing marriage? So, I took it for granted. I was 34 years old and never been in so much trouble in my whole life. I was no stranger to it, though, but because I was going through heartbreak, I could have cared less!

See, this all happened when my ex-husband and I were going through financial hardships, and both of our parents had cancer; my ex-husband was not paying the bills due to the loss of his job because of the big oil spill. And of course, he was chasing other women, partying, and hanging out with his drug dealer friends all while I was taking care of my ill father, so money was low. One day I had the bright idea when my dad dropped his morphine pill to swipe his medication and sell it for a few dollars, something I'm not very proud of. At this point, I did not know that the narcotics task force was after my ex-husband and his friends watching their every move, which included mine. While leaving the neighborhood, the police got behind me in an unmarked car. I did not think much of it until the blue lights came on, and I was pulled over. I forgot that I had a morphine pill in my purse, and when they searched my vehicle, I was arrested for narcotics possession and had to be bonded out after a few days of sitting in the local county jail.

So, my ex-husband and I hired an attorney, which in my opinion, was not a very good one! I decided to take probation and thought I could handle it. After completion, I was told that I would be non-adjudicated, meaning once completed, it would be off my record. So, I took it! Another big mistake on my part! During this point in my life, I let my emotions rule over my common-sense big time. Probation seemed easy just report every month and pay your fines; this was supposed to go on for three years. But during this time in my life, I was at my worst. My ex-husband decided to leave me for a drug-addicted prostitute sending me into an intense depression. Suicidal thoughts and homicidal feelings were the only things on my mind. Probation, unfortunately, was the last on the list.

After not reporting for several months, I became an absconder meaning "a person on the run," not my intentions but try telling the justice system that! Eventually, I was caught, and I was a mess. I'm sure God saved me at this point in my life from myself and from being around the wrong people, who could potentially have had me drugged out, getting new felony charges, or worse, being murdered! I was caught up in the drugged-out coast world full of cartels, mafias, gangs, junkies, and roguish-like characters. That will have you thanking God you escaped with your mind and life.

So, during my revocation hearing (probation violation), I was sentenced to prison for my failure to comply with my probation conditions and was now adjudicated. Goodbye, good record, and hello, Felon!

While shackled on a cramped bus for two uncomfortable hours, all I could do was pray and ask myself, "Where has my life taken me?"

I pondered on this for quite some time during my incarceration. We finally reached our destination at Mississippi Correctional Facility; I was out of my element. "I cannot believe I'm here," I said to myself, shaking my head in disbelief.

I cannot say I was scared; I have always been very much a tough cookie throughout my life, more like surprised that I landed myself in Hell. It was dark and gloomy. You saw happy women, sad women, strange women, just all sorts of women. A bunch of women who like me made poor decisions, whether it was their fault or someone else's fault. There were murderers, child abusers, drug dealers, drug users, money launders, thieves, drunk drivers, scam artists, and probation violators. No one's crime better than another, and we were treated the same. We were all criminals.

There are some things that you will as a human being will never get accustomed to and somethings you will never forget. I was horrified at having to bend over and squat while having strangers looking up inside of my lady parts, but what could I really do? Learning to accept things were about to be part of the normalcy in my life for a year or so, like bathing with other women standing next to you, using the bathroom as someone else sits next to you on their commode legs almost touching. Nothing in the world could prepare you for prison life; you learn how to adapt to your surroundings quicker than others.

Although my experience was shorter than most of the women in prison, it seemed like I was there forever! I was released in time to witness my daughter's first prom; as humans, we sometimes tend to lose focus on what is important in our lives. We become so consumed in our own pain while neglecting the ones around us. Relearning how to be Veronica again was a long process, and that took time and understanding from my friends and family, even myself.

Between ankle monitors and probation, my process to become who I was meant to be during and after was not without pain and strife; learning to adjust and revamp a better me was far from my hardest task but well worth the fight. I never wanted to experience my freedom taking away from me again. I never wanted another Human being to be the director of my life; I had to take charge of my own life. I eventually Divorced after ten hurtful years of abuse, infidelity, lies, and mental anguish.

During my readjustment, I leveled up as one of the coast's most popular bartenders/bar managers in the casinos, restaurants, local bars, and clubs. I eventually started studying and gluing myself and attention to my studies, and started learning herbology, spirituality, chakra healing, soap making, jewelry making, and business planning. And eventually felt confident and opened my own business. Getting my business license has been one of the proudest moments in my life; not only did it teach me I am more than my past, but it taught me I am the only one that can make me happy, and despite my turbulent life, I can make changes. Authentic and unapologetically, I learned to change my surroundings; I am still the girl with the tattoos and gold teeth, not ashamed of my past "we all have one," I am just a better version of her, and she refuses to be behind any more locked doors!

About Veronica McGee

Veronica "Vee" McGee is a mixologist, spiritual coach, mentor, and herbalist in women's health. She is the CEO and founder of Lotus Moon Holistic and Spiritual Gifts, LLC; where, she is branding new products constantly in her growing business. After finishing high school, a teen mom, she ventured out to try various different career fields such as: beautician, medical receptionist/CNA, and bartender. With a great family support system, she could explore all but never quite found her passion.

Born in Colorado Springs on October 5, 1979, her parents where military which made her a resident of many places such as Louisiana, Florida, Japan, and finally residing permanently in Biloxi, MS. After High school she lived in Texas, Delaware, Arizona, and St. Louis but always returned to the Gulf Coast. Veronica has a passion for such causes as Teen Pregnancy where she worked with the Mayor of Ocean Springs, MS mentoring young teens on the woes of being a teen mom. She is a mother of 3, grandmother, wife, daughter, sister, aunt, and

CEO. You will find that her perseverance over her life challenges never swayed her from being the best version of herself.

E-mail: <u>Veenaturalyme55@gmail.com</u>
Facebook: @lotusmoonvee

The Life Path Chosen for Me

by Sher Graham

Destiny. Gifts. Transformation.

The Lord is my Shepherd, I shall not want." – Psalms 23:1

*H*ave you ever met yourself going in the opposite direction? I am paid to write and speak. As a lifelong storyteller, I have written stories about other people, places and companies. I help communities, raise money for charity, plan successful events, and empower others to create their dreams. Some of my friends/clients are famous, wealthy, and the 'go-to expert'. As "Fairy Godmother," I create calm from chaos!

I walked through hell during my unauthentic life journey, taking twists and turns into the depth of betrayal, despair, confusion, unworthiness, and not really knowing who I was to bring me on my walk past hell. Then I finally met the **'real'** authentic me at age 65.

I wrote my script, directed my life path, starred as lead actor, and created the responses to all the 'ACTION' plots, stunts, and illusions seen in the film. The low budget film was a box office sensation. There was a scene each movie attendee could relate to, shaking their head and saying aloud **"THAT IS ME."**

To become the real ME, I thank: my grandmothers for their love reminding me God is first, you can't buy love with money and giving me a legacy of sharing with others; my quiet grandfathers for hugs and their time; my 'second Moms/Dads' - Mom K/Dad L, Mom F/ Dad H; Mom K/ Dad G who knew the issue; family members who understood my truth; ; my teachers; my friends/tribe who have supported me with love, prayers, dancing and music!.

Finally, I thank my parents for giving me so many opportunities **with conditions,** for not understanding who I was, nor what I dreamed of doing/becoming, nor showing me unconditional love and support. Being sensitive is a gift; insensitive sarcasm is not a gift. And most of all, for **not** walking in my shoes while my mother's undiagnosed pre-scriptive opioid use (substance abuse disorder) fractured relationships throughout my life. It only strengthened my faith in God; He is the only Father I need to please at the end of the day. For these things, I am grateful. Thank you for teaching me 'who not to become" - insensitive words and actions, verbal abuse, bullying, disrespect through my adult-hood – the foundation of my trauma.

Destiny

October 19, 1951. Life began the day I was born. From inside my mother's womb, I cried out after I hustled my way to the light. *Would I have chosen to be in the light of this loving couple had I known what the journey would become over the course of the next few decades?* Of course. This is the journey God and the universe had destined for me. Who was I to not take the first step out into the world? Step taken. Carry on.

My mother's undiagnosed substance abuse disorder from pre-scriptive drugs/opioids from during her lifetime went unnoticed by neighbors, church, community, and supported by the doctors who wrote her prescriptions. Yet, I saw the changes in her behavior. I knew from an early age that she needed help, and no one was listening. Where was my father and brother through her years of struggle and deception? They were there.

Her daily tantrums resulted in her negative and abusive behavior towards me, her friends, strangers in stores and people she did not even know. Sometimes I became her parent when behaviors became embarrassing.

My mother's co-occurring undiagnosed mental disorder - hypo-chondria or health anxiety (Somatic Symptom Disorder) - presents itself when a person is continuously concerned about any physical or psycho-logical symptoms they detect, no matter how minor the symptom may be, and are convinced that they have, or are about to be diagnosed with, a serious illness.

Her perceived physical challenges were continuous and overlapped each other with her conviction that she was ill. I passionately believe that the self-talk we speak to ourselves, our mind shares with our body that responds to the message. If you continue to tell yourself you have something wrong, it can lead to that illness showing up. (Yes, we do have legitimate illnesses that can impede our health, but mind, body and soul work together as we walk through the journey of health.)

My conversations with my mother about well-being, self-worth, and manipulation resulted in the manifestation of serious illnesses, outbursts of hurtful comments, and love with conditions. My mother was an intelligent woman and manipulator.

I could never tell what prescription she was taking for what illness written by which doctor. In 1988, I found out that doctors in our community did not know she was being treated by other colleagues and she had self-medicated for decades. Her own denial came in the form of her 'meds' being allergy pills and that drinking alcohol did not affect her drugs.

When you have one parent in denial about their drug addiction and the other parent in denial about being an enabler and about the addiction, communication or lack of within the household and family becomes toxic and nonexistent.

What I can share with you is that our relationship was very unhealthy and traumatizing for decades. I learned after my brother was born in 1955 that my mother wanted a boy as her first child, and God gave me to her. The unconditional love I thought was there from each parent was never really expressed in "I love you", "I am proud of you." Conditional love was the trajectory of communications that would shape my life journey.

My mother's own insecurity and lack of self-worth caused her to make irrational decisions. As a child, she gave me part of her valium right before a recital. Years later, my body spoke to me when I developed chemical/food/environmental sensitivities. I listened. I am alive.

My early accomplishments made me happy: playing the piano, singing, and dancing; published author (age 10); typed fast, wrote press releases to my local newspaper promoting my volunteer activities. I bowled in leagues, won awards. I excelled in writing, won awards. By age 17, I was a special populations activist and lobbied at the Ohio State House. My first business at age 10 was a babysitting service; first entrepreneurial venture at age 17 continued the oval cycle of my business today.

BUT! *For each positive experience, there was a condition.* Life according to my mother: my singing and piano were off-key (she was tone deaf); my writing was written by someone else; married/divorced twice; mismanaged money. Yes, I made poor choices in male relationships, always 'looking for love in all the wrong places." Money had always been there; so, no connection or appreciation by me. Yet, all I really wanted was a hug without conditions, authentic approval – unconditional love.

It is the early patterning of behavioral communications between my family members that created my trauma. I know now I am responsible/accountable for each choice I made and continue to make. My faith and trust in God have carried me so many times. I persevered. Carry on.

Gifts

My gifts were enlightened in mind, body, and spirit with everything I read, and stored away in my memory. I felt wise beyond my years in one way but knew there was much to learn. My gifts defied each other; confused, unrealistic avoiding my gifts of empath, intuition, creativity, and compassion. No one knew I was Indigo child.

A photographic memory, clairaudient hearing, gift of healing and connecting with spirit on many levels and many forms, and an intuitive gift of 'just knowing'. A gift of empath, highly creative, and yet logical thinking at a high-functioning level. God saw it all happen. He was always there, even when I was not always following His design.

Transformation

What is my transformation? "O Lord, for You have lifted me up." (Psalms 30:1)

- God and the universe are higher energy and a more powerful vibration than any person or thing on earth.

- My choices, my behavior, my gratitude, my gifts, my life journey are mine.

- Communications in all forms (including God's humor) are key to positive, successful outcomes and guides me through the path I take to overcome my obstacles. Be real with ME first about me.

- Authenticity is important with everyone in my daily influencer circle. My actions speak louder than my words to the people and communities I serve.

- My tribe gives me the strength to persevere, twirl, and carry on when I change course to create calm from chaos!

- Failure is a gift; learn from it. Teach others how not to end with same results.

- Celebrate the small achievements every day. Speak your truth.

- The vibrations you set forth in the world will guide the vibrational energy of others.

I AM ENOUGH. I am still learning. I am still living. It is my voice that is now heard. A new day, a new journey has begun.

About Sher Graham

Change is the only constant in Sher Graham's life journey! A business-woman of 50 years, she uses her storytelling gifts (writing and speaking) to coach, guide, consult, educate individuals and companies. Her experience as a behavioral health communications scientist in human behavior, system dynamics, and communications, plus her empath intuition, helps others achieve happiness, joy, peace, calm, become organized, and fulfilling their dreams. Sher is the Executive Vice President, Behavioral Health/Organizational Communications, OSBI/Synergy Solutions Collaborative in Mobile, AL. Graham is a business/education/nonprofit consultant; executive trainer and international speaker (7,000 presentations); community activist/volunteer (100,000+ hours); and award-winning writer/journalist/columnist/poet/author.

A native Ohioan and Kent State University (Ohio) graduate (B.S. Education/Speech Communications), she co-chairs the Gulf Coast Mental Health Coalition, and serves on national and local nonprofit boards.

"Words became my life at age 10 when I was first published." Now, she writes for her voice. Sher shares her own story of trauma, resilience, synergy and perseverance with humor and life lessons learned, hoping others will hear and make better choices. Her current writings include her autobiography, an inspirational series and a business case study.

Sher Graham
Business website: www.shergraham.com
Email: slgraham4969@gmail.com

I Didn't See It Coming

by Felicia Long

Dysfunction in the family is a problem that we all have, but so many people do not recognize that this problem exists. They are in denial! Do you know any families like this? Well, let me tell you my story.

My tragic incident happened on March 21st, 2018 at 4:30 a.m. right after my morning prayer. It was the day before I was to have my second surgery on my left knee replacement that I had one year prior. I walked into the kitchen to take out food for dinner and the enemy attacked hard. His influence came through my younger child who was staying with me for the fifth time because she and her child had been displaced.

She had just finished ironing his clothes for school and she made a remark that struck me! She said, "You are always messing with other people's food!" In my mind, I was being motherly and thought I would cook for everyone. Well, that did not sit well with her because the meat was hers. We always shared food, but all hell broke loose. You see, my body was already weak from four major spinal surgeries which left me with 150 staples to my stomach and back because of a collapsing spine. I had no plans of arguing, let alone, fighting my own child! I was always taught to be obedient to your parents so that your days may be long upon this earth (Ephesians 6:1).

However, when she began to use profanity and started to tongue-lash me, I lost control of my own emotions. It didn't dawn on me that the iron was still hot! So, I picked it up and slammed her against the refrigerator door and drew back my hand with the iron to hit her with it. You see, my mom always frowned against disobedient children. Whenever we got out of line with her, whatever was in her reach she picked it up and hit us with it, even if we were a distance away and it had to boomerang to find us!

Well, of course, she blocked the hit but the laugh she gave was taunting. And then she overpowered me, and we tumbled and fell on top of my kitchen table knocking it to the floor and words were being exchanged. I can't tell you what they were, but it wasn't Christian tongues, it was more than likely my original set of tongues that weren't tamed!

I could feel a sting, but it didn't occur to me that this child had burned me four times with this hot iron. I had a huge burn on my right shoulder, the side of the iron print alongside my neck, a burn mark on my eyelid and above my brow. As the incident was taking place, my granddaughter came out of her room and got photo evidence with her phone for the police.

The police were called and, as usual, they didn't take her to jail, but they did call the paramedics who transferred me 50 miles from home to a burn trauma center, where I received some ointment, bandages and was told to follow up with my primary care physician. Upon returning home, I walked straight through the door and the peace of God fell upon me. It was a peace that I had never felt before. She was sitting on the couch in a sorrowful state, something I had never seen from her. As I walked into my room, my granddaughter showed me the pictures of the incident. When I saw the photo, tears started to stream down my face in disbelief of how distorted her face was while she was burning me. I felt pity for myself and for her because it could have been the other way around. I began to feel angry, and I heard the Lord say, "You have to show forgiveness, just like I have forgiven you. No matter what you have done, you must also show that to her and walk in it." He further stated, "I know you don't want to, and it might not always be easy, but do it anyway." I knew I couldn't do this of my own accord, so I murmured, "Lord, show me how."

I am glad that I changed my thoughts of anger because if I pondered too long, I would have given a place to the devil. So, I kept my mouth shut and remembered the words of the Lord. One day, she walked into my room and said, "Mom, can I talk to you?" as she sat on my bed. She began to cry and said, "I am sorry. I didn't know that I burnt you that bad." I asked, "But why did you pick up the hot iron? Why did you burn me? I would have rather for you to have knocked the iron out of my hand and just went outside." I further reminded her that she knew I didn't like children, grown or not, disrespecting their parents and that my ill emotions took over. And, yes, it could have been avoided because I initiated the fight and for that, I am sorry, and I forgive you (even though I knew I wanted to hurt her at the time). She said, "Mom, you always taught me to defend myself." I said, "Yes, but not against me."

As I write this story today, I am not mad at all - even though we broke the code, and we defiled the honor between a mother and a daughter. We were really trying to get our relationship back on track because we had been at odds many times and she would throw up in my face, seemingly bragging, how she burnt me. I had to hold my peace, even if I had to take a deep breath, or walk away. I had to do that for myself! I saw her at my aunt's home going celebration and that peace that I needed came upon me again. I saw her hugging a relative and I began hugging them both. She said, "No ma'am, I am not going to disrespect you, but we are not cool like that." I said, "Maybe not, but I still love you." And, she said, "I love you, too." and I walked away in the calmness of that peace.

The lesson that I have learned throughout this whole experience is that the bible says, as I paraphrase, we are like Jesus as a sheep led to be slaughtered (Acts 8:32) and the most powerful truth of the matter is that I have to love my neighbor and enemies, learn to relax, release, let go and let God handle all my affairs. The forgiveness was not so much for her as it was for me because I know that if I don't learn to master it, then this harmful spirit can take control and cause all sorts of havoc to my mind, spirit, and body, which can lead to physical health conditions. The bible says in Proverbs 4:23 "Keep thy heart with all diligence; for out of it are the issues of life."

Therefore, if I am to avoid any situation of any magnitude that could negatively affect me, that I have to do as the bible says in Ephesians 6:11 "Put on the whole armour of God, that ye may be able to stand against the wiles of the devil." I know that I cannot let a day go where I don't do my morning prayer and devotions. I read the word of God, praise, and worship with songs, and even do a dance or two. I do some fasting to keep my flesh under subject and I watch what I allow into my spirit through my eyes and ears. These are strategies that if I let slip by, then I would have let my guard down and open myself up for unwanted entry of potential danger.

About Felicia Long

Felicia Yvette Long in a gravitating shifting world that is ever evolving in cycles and seasons is a fierce, fiery young lady who is outspoken with integrity and dignity. Although she has some disabilities, she is not disqualified. She keeps it real, raw, and truthful with no sugar coating. Her physical limitations have caused her to use the rich mind and wisdom that the Lord has blessed her with.

She is a five-time published author with three books being anthologies and two solo of her own. She is a speaker, preacher and teacher of the Word of God and have preached on The Way Television which aired on seven continents and 150 cities.

Felicia's academic achievements include a Bachelor of Science in Human Service and a Master of Business Administration from the University of Phoenix and she has graduated from The Sonship School of the First Born in Victorville, Ca. She is also the founder of Global

Warfare Ministries and host of The Anointed Fire Prayer line. As a contributor to society, she supports Feed the Children and St. Jude for cancer research.

E-mail: hilefavored@hotmail.com
E-mail: elderfylong@gmail.com

It Was Only A Test

by Cheryl Kehl

The day I found myself with my three kids hiding in a phone booth with sticks as guns on Naval Weapons Station Earle in Colts Neck, New Jersey, was the beginning of my test. I was in the emergency room being examined by a doctor and did not realize how I got there. This was when I found out I had a temporary nervous breakdown. This small part of my story tells what lead to that day that the enemy could have stolen my mind. I was recently released from active duty from the United States Navy and was married to a Navy Yeoman. During the years of our marriage, he was cheating and having children with other women. I found out that he grew up in a home where his mother was dealing with domestic violence, so he thought that was normal. We fought a lot, and I say fight because if he laid hands on me, I laid hands back on him. It was nothing for us weekly to have the military police, chaplain, EMTs, and Officer on duty at our home. We fought so much they made him move out of base housing and into the barracks.

I was stuck on base without a job, car, or home phone and away from my family. I only knew the lady next door – who I found out was also cheating on her husband *with* my husband. So, then I found myself with no one I could trust. I had family about 4 hours away, but I did not want to burden anyone and was trying to figure out what I could do to help myself. After joining the Navy, I divorced my ex-husband and did not want to look like I was failing again with another marriage. So, I was trying to hide from my family what was going on. I knew too many people with happy marriages, so I could not understand why I was such a failure.

Right after my husband moved out of our home, he would send his friend over to make sure we did not need anything. I thought that was a very nice gesture since we were not on speaking terms. During the third visit, his friend brought dinner over for the kids and me. He also brought drinks over. I did not realize that I was drinking too much and became cloudy. His friend decided to rape me that night. I called my husband's aunt, who drove five hours to come to see about me. We decided to contact the military police, and a report was taken, and I was advised to go to medical to be examined. Little did I know that I would not be looked out for even when a crime took place as a civilian.

Right in the middle of the rape, domestic violence, one of my first cousins was beaten badly and was placed on life support. At this point, a family member came and picked us up to be with family. I was told by the military that since I decided to leave that it did not seem like I was raped. What a crazy thing to say to a person because they decided to be with a family member who was on life support. After my cousin passed away and we had the funeral, I went back to my home on the base to try and figure out how to handle everything that took place. After one week, this was too much for my mind to deal with, and I decided to take a break and shut down.

I continued to have my husband come by the house and ask that we try and work it out. I was too weak mentally to not agree, and he moved back in. The fights started again, but this time I did not call anyone until I thought day and night about killing him and tried to figure out how not to get caught. I decided to go to the base counselors because I was again starting to feel like I was getting close to losing my mind. I was raised in the church and gave my life to Christ at the age of 13, so I knew that I was in a backslidden state and needed to find my way back to God. Being abandoned was something that I knew all too well. When I was a child my brother and I was given to my grandparent to be raised by my mother. I was a secret child that my mother had by a married man, so he did not publicly claim me as a child. So, in my mind, this husband was abandoning me just like everyone else. This was a little different, though, because he wanted to beat on me too.

I was convinced by the counselor on the base to get out fast while he was at work. She suggested I go to a battered women's shelter. I agreed and was given 45 minutes to go back to the house and get what

I thought we needed for 60 days. Oh, I forgot to tell you I found out the week before that I was pregnant with my fourth child. Off to the shelter, we went for what I thought would be 60 days, which turned into 90 days. I met many women at that time who suffered a lot at the hands of their abusers. I heard horrific stories and knew that God had spared me some. I would talk to woman after woman learning their story for reasons unknown until years later. After 90 days, I was given rental assistance and moved back near my family. The rental assistance and welfare allowed me to start my life back over on my own.

After making more mistakes with more men, I decided to find a church and tell God I was ready to live on His terms. I begin realizing that the temporary breakdown could have been the day that I mentally crossed over and never returned. I begin to understand that yes, I had a walk past hell, but God spared me from entering into hell. I decided that everything that the devil put on me those years I would use for ministry. So, I begin volunteering at the battered women's shelter and being there for those ladies. I also became a Rape Crisis Counselor and would go to the emergency room and be with rape victims during their examination and while being interviewed by the police. I look at all the things that I have been through in my life was for me to be able to understand and be there for other women.

I have had too many things happen that contributed to my walk past hell to tell in one chapter. But the beauty of the story is that God allowed me to make it through those difficult times. I found out I was stronger than I ever imagined I could be. I have learned to be an understanding ear for those who have gone through similar situations. I understand that I am the Woman of God I am today because of my experiences. I am blessed because so many women were in abusive relationships that stayed way too long. Some did not make it out to tell their story. One of these ladies includes my God sister Audrey Joyce, who was murdered by her ex. I think about my friend who wanted me to partner with her in helping women in the church who was experiencing abuse and a shame to tell anyone. It took years for me to find out that she was one of those women who was preaching the gospel every week but was being beaten at home and made to sleep on the porch with no coat in the wintertime.

I am currently completing a Domestic Violence Advocacy program because I will no longer hide my story. I want to help others do the same to speak up and speak out. I want other women to be able to move forward in their life and allow the healing process to begin. I decided some years ago to get healed so I could minister to women and not from a broken place but a healed place. If you are reading this chapter and want the healing to begin, please find me on social media I have walked past hell and want to help women find their peace. I believe the heat from hell lit the flame for me to live freer, soar higher, and gave me a burning desire to go after the things that God places in my heart. Be Free!

About Cheryl Kehl

A world filled with stronger family units, support the much-needed ethics of generational prosperity, healing, and communal and global reconciliation. Leading the way by example, is the compassionate advocate, Cheryl Kehl.

Cheryl Kehl is an author, cleric, business generalist, and a faith-based family coach, with a heart for broken women and domestic violence victims, facing substantial difficulties due to a history of diverse traumas. Moved deeply by her faith in God, Cheryl is a certified Christian life, intimacy, and relationship professional, in the business of seeing women reinstate healthy boundaries, enter into loving marriages, and sustain growing families, rooted in a relationship with Christ.

Cheryl's mantra is simple: she wants to reach women who have experienced hardships in life and bring them into an understanding that they can pick up and use what the devil meant for evil, to further the Kingdom of God.

Cheryl's love for domestic reconciliation, is accommodated by a regard for higher learning; as she has received both, a Master of Arts – Business Administration from the University of Phoenix and a Bachelor of Arts in Business Administration; with a concentration in Organizational Management, from Edward Waters College in Jacksonville, Florida. Cheryl is also a certified property and sales expert, giving her the ability to properly convey to families, the importance of home ownership.

When Cheryl is not out volunteering and mentoring both women and families, she currently serves as a Chaplain to women at the Duval County Detention Center and looks forward to being certified as a Domestic Violence H.E.L.P. Coach, this spring. Inspired inherently by the people she meets every day, Cheryl is seen as a beloved member of her local community, a wife, mother, and cherished friend.

Cheryl Kehl. Leader. | Organizer. | Advocate.
E-mail: cherylkehl@gmail.com
Contact number: 904-382-3238.

Made in the USA
Middletown, DE
24 May 2022